97
101
111
117
120
122
137
151
154 *

Creating
a New
World
Politics

Creating a New World Politics

from conflict to cooperation

DAVID V. EDWARDS
University of Texas at Austin

David McKay Company, Inc.   New York

To Marjorie Van Deusen Edwards
and Carrie Allen Edwards,
with admiration and love

An Acknowledgment

This book was provoked by the state of the world and the state of criticism of it—especially the emergence of a new conventional wisdom that things international will improve significantly if only we reorder our priorities and curtail our commitments. My dissatisfaction with this view—whether it be expressed by Senate doves or by the Nixon Doctrine—matches my disaffection with the present international situation and the policies responsible for it, as will become readily apparent to the reader.

Most of this book, which attempts to provide a promising alternative, was written at the Washington Center of Foreign Policy Research, which proved once again to be a provocatively mined harbor away from my usual academic ocean, the University of Texas. I am especially grateful to the University of Texas Research Institute for the grant that made the year of research and writing possible, to Robert E. Osgood, Director of the Washington Center of Foreign Policy Research, for his invitation to spend the year at the Center, to Elaine Clark of the Center, for help that facilitated preparation of the first draft of the manuscript in various ways, and to Edward Artinian, my editor at David McKay, for his interest and efforts on behalf of the book, which I hope have only just begun as I write this.

I have received extensive helpful comments on the manuscript from Robert J. Lieber, Charles J. Parrish, Karl M. Schmitt, and Summer Scott, as well as encouragement from Frank Beer, Robert C. Gray, Russell Hardin, and a number of my students, and general stimulation from my colleague Roderick Bell. I thank all of them for their readings and responses, while claiming the greater part of responsibility for this work nonetheless. Other significant influences upon my thinking are indicated in the concluding "Note on Sources, Influences, and Further Pursuits."

I hope that others, too, will read and respond. The problems that I, like so many others, am wrestling with will not submit to anything less than a collective and increasingly cooperative campaign. I hope we will all construct that essential venture, in order to create a new world politics.

DAVID V. EDWARDS
Austin, Texas
May 1972

Contents

A Prologue

The immediate reaction to President Richard M. Nixon's visits to Peking and Moscow was a widespread combination of hope and relief. To some it seemed the capstone of his efforts to make possible, if not to secure, the "generation of peace" of which he had so frequently spoken. To others less optimistic, the various agreements that emerged during the visits—especially the Strategic Arms Limitation (SALT) agreements—seemed at least to indicate that progress in pacifying relations between hostile Great Powers could be arranged—at least within limits.

Popular reactions of euphoria and expert reactions of optimism are the common consequence of the periodic manifestations of apparent progress in international relations. In this sense, the Spirit of Peking and the Spirit of Moscow are no different from the Spirit of Geneva or the Spirit of Vienna or the Spirit of Glassboro. Each is a manifestation, in both the public and the leadership, of the hope that greater peace and extended progress are possible. These Spirits usually prove ephemeral at best, being followed by a renewed deterioration in Great Power relations. And this eventual failure serves only to reinforce—paradoxically, perhaps—the other critical effect of such optimism and euphoria: a renewed confidence in the reliance on the old, the traditional, ways of understanding and conducting international relations.

Thus when the President reported to Congress on his visit to Moscow, he praised the Congress for having previously rejected efforts to cut back or eliminate the antiballistic missile (ABM) system that he himself had just limited, asserting that "The time-tested policies of vigilance and firmness which have brought us to this summit are the ones that can safely carry us forward to further progress in reaching agreements to reduce the danger of war."

This "lesson" of international relations and the concomitant assessment of the Moscow visit and the SALT agreements is typical. Unfortunately, it seems all too likely that the eventual effects of these agreements too will be typical. Arms control agreements, however they are "sold" to the American people—whether for their asserted contribution to our security or for their possible economic benefits as limitations on the skyrocketing cost of military hardware—tend eventually to founder on the desperate faith in reliance on military force.

This dependence on the military approach to national security and international order, which is characteristic of all major states at this time, generates—indeed, compels—overcompensation by governments for the possible effects of the limitations reached. Thus when President John F. Kennedy achieved the ban on atmospheric nuclear testing in 1963, he immediately pledged that he would quickly intensify underground nuclear testing. And when President Nixon returned from Moscow, aides lost no time assuring the military and exhorting the Congress that we would intensify development of the major offensive weapons systems not limited by the agreements.

Such usual efforts are not generally justified, as skeptics may believe, because they will result in new military advantages for the country—although the underground testing, for example, did make possible improvement of the warheads for the ABM systems that the Moscow agreements eventually limited as well as development of the Multiple Independently-targetable Reentry Vehicles (MIRVs) that the Moscow agreements significantly *did not* limit. Rather, hypertrophic development of those new weapons systems that are not prohibited is always justified as a protection against the possibility that the other side will develop the systems and hence gain an advantage if we don't do likewise. In addition, such further development and deployment is justified as providing "bargaining chips" for the possible next round of arms control talks, on the questionable assumption that you cannot limit anything until you have it or are doing it.

Thus what happens in and after arms control agreements is a good example of a phenomenon we all know well in international relations: the self-confirming "preparation-for-the-worst" that has been at the root of the cold war arms race between the United States and the Soviet Union since the end of the Second World War.

Everyone knows that this is self-defeating, even if—or indeed *especially if*—it works as intended and expected. As a result of the arms race created by each side's preparing for the worst the other could do, each side is poorer economically because of the wastage of resources on arms and the distortions of the national economy that result. In addition, each side may well be less secure as a result of the increased danger of war by accident with new weapons systems, as well as by the new dangers created, for example, by ABM systems that threaten to destabilize the deterrent balance defensively, or by MIRV systems that threaten to destabilize it offensively.

But while everyone in leadership in each of the Great Powers knows that this approach is self-defeating, *each feels trapped or forced into adopting it anyway*—even when, as now seems to be the case—each wants to live at peace and even perhaps in harmony with the others.

Some have sought to explain this paradoxical situation in terms of the impact of the military on policy making, or of party political competition, or of the vested interests of what is often referred to, in language first used popularly by President Dwight D. Eisenhower in a "farewell address" a dozen years ago, as "the military-industrial complex." But what is most important in determining that each state follows this self-defeating course is the beliefs and fears of the leaders—and, often, the publics—that there is no available alternative, that the nature of international reality requires it.

But is this self-defeating, repeating resort to military postures and approaches to political problems inescapable—even in a world and at a time when a president whose political career was built upon intense anti-Communism can go to Peking and Moscow in a pronounced spirit of friendship and cooperation?

The answer is *no*. But that answer, and the bases for it, have obviously still escaped that president, as they have continued to escape most major political leaders and analysts. Fragments of the answer, as we have already begun to see and shall see much more clearly in the pages to come, are increasingly obvious even to political leaders "trained" in and by a very different world. But the necessary fundamental understanding of international relations is not yet quite at hand.

We must come to recognize and appreciate the revolutionary promise of a better understanding of several critical features of international relations as they are evolving.

First, we must recognize that policy makers and pundits alike have generally agreed on the fundamental nature and requirements of international reality. Consequently, what have been presented and debated as promising fundamental alternatives to the dominant approach—such as the currently voguish appeal for commitment-cutting and priority-reordering—are not really significantly different from present policy and the understanding on which it is based.

Next, we must discover and understand how this general agreement (and the concomitant offering of alternatives that are not really alternatives) defeats policies and programs—such as the arms control measures we have cited above—by enabling processes—the wrong processes—to dominate policy, and by nurturing a reliance upon force and the threat of force as the primary instrument of policy that is called for and validated essentially by its own self-defeating effects.

Third, we must develop an understanding of this problem that can incorporate—as a first step toward its solution—a changed consciousness of what we shall term "the social creation of reality," the process by which our assumptions about the nature of international reality drastically affect that international reality over time.

Fourth, we must uncover and project the fundamental trends in national and international politics and society that promise fundamental transformations in the bases and possibilities of international relations—changes we will be able to encourage and exploit once we anticipate them.

And finally, we must discover how we might devise an American foreign policy designed to begin reconstruction of international relations so that they are less violent and more cooperative, so that they contribute increased welfare rather than "illfare" to the peoples of the world. This needed new American foreign policy must be constructive, must be increasingly capable of inducing reciprocation by other states (especially the Soviet Union), and must above all be designed to limit the role of force in international relations and thereby vitiate the mutually self-defeating militarized foreign policies which the states and their leaders still feel themselves compelled to maintain.

It is this progression that we shall follow in this essay designed to contribute to the understanding and imagination that alone can offer a real opportunity for creating a New World Politics.

PART ONE

The
United States
in the World Crisis

chapter one

International Relations as Continuing Catastrophe

On International Relations

No one aware of the unending disaster of Vietnam, the extended torment of the Middle East, the tragedy of Czechoslovakia, and the catastrophes of Biafra, Bangladesh, and so many other states needs to be reminded of the continuing unsatisfactory state of international relations in this third decade since the end of the bloodiest war in mankind's history. No one with any but the narrowest concept of self-interest for our nation needs an analysis of the unsatisfactory ways in which the interests of other peoples and our interests for other peoples remain unattended, or are attended in ways that produce the opposite of their and our desires. And no one viewing our internal problems of poverty and racial antagonism, pollution and crime, and alienation and animosity needs reminder that we spend less in attention and resources on our basic internal needs and challenges than we all agree should be spent.

The greatest source of dissatisfaction with the nature of, or quality of, international relations is probably the high violence content—both violence manifest and violence threatened —in relations among adversaries, whether they be superpow-

3

ers or breakaway portions of new, weak states. The prevalence and prominence of violence intensifies two critical feelings: anxiety over the high cost of the failure to maintain peaceable relations among states; and despair over the increasing uncontrollability of affairs, not merely between other pairs of lesser states, as in the Middle East, but also between our state and its major adversaries.

Furthermore, this discomfort is compounded for those who place significant value upon the extension of freedom of choice and action to the newer states and to their peoples, and those who place high value upon the sharing of resources among the haves and the have-nots. For neither of these overlapping groups of advocates, the first of which certainly includes all those responsible for the creation and conduct of American foreign policy in the years since 1945, and the second of which certainly includes the major elements of the peace movement and in fact most businessmen desiring greater international commercial opportunities—neither of these groups can find much in today's international affairs to reassure it that freedom is growing and welfare is spreading around the world. And we see many indications that much of international relations as now practiced tends to vitiate efforts at such progress, whether it be the actual effects of the Vietnam war that was allegedly designed to improve life for the peasantry, or the effects of assistance to both sides in the Middle Eastern conflict that was intended to stabilize relations so that development could take place on both sides and the conflict could recede in importance and decline in virulence. And, indeed, even the once-supposed success stories such as the political and economic development of Nigeria have turned to chaos and virtual genocide as the superpowers either stood by unable to be influences for peace, or intervened only to see their efforts exacerbate disaster.

Of course, where pessimism reigns, these recollections,

far from being appreciated, are assailed as foolish and even dangerous. Some believe that progress which might be noticed and applauded—that is, progress greater than the years since 1945 have seen—is not possible. But few beyond some of those responsible for policy in this period share this assessment. Most can produce suggestions—especially ex post facto —of how the United States might have improved the world by altering its policy, perhaps by a firmer stand on Laotian affairs in 1962, perhaps by a more conciliatory posture toward Castro's Cuba or Mao's China at one or another point. And, as we well know, some strong critics propose U.S. withdrawal around the world as promising a major improvement.

Nonetheless, even the pessimists seem committed to the notion that things will improve. It is difficult to develop and maintain a policy without a belief that it will effect improvement—at least for a self-pronounced superpower. And this very fact seems to convince many that progress is indeed made. Thus we often hear "the prevention of nuclear war since 1945" cited not simply as a notable achievement but as an indicator of real progress or improvement. But we also know that nuclear proliferation increasingly threatens and that we have had too many smaller wars. The overall level of violence in our international system seems very high, and the "illfare" of the peoples of the less developed countries seems more pronounced as the industrialized states develop further. And to compound our problems, the international system shows no susceptibility whatsover to our growing concerns about the environment—concerns that are consummately international in effect as well as increasingly multinational in cause.

The trends we perceive—among them nuclear proliferation, spreading arms races, the weakening of extraction economies, displacement of new and less authoritarian regimes, increase in new and smaller states—cannot be viewed with equanimity, even by those who expect little visible progress in international relations.

But these failures and dangers are all too familiar, and the quality of international relations is all too clear. The important question is not, What is wrong with international relations? Rather, the important question is, What can be done to improve the quality of international relations? And in order to uncover and develop promising new answers to that crucial question, we must first discover not only why international relations are and have for so long been disastrous, but also why the policy makers and scholars who have sought to devise new and promising approaches to improvement in the past have been unable to succeed and have often exacerbated an already bad situation. The answers to these questions are certainly not obvious, for there has been an extensive consensus among most foreign policy experts during the years since 1945 over the range of available measures and how promising each was in given circumstances. Thus we must first examine the shape of the continuing debate over possible reform of international relations briefly to discover what differences there have been and what possibilities have been proposed. Only then will we be able to discover what possibilities have not been seriously considered and why, and to ask whether the surprising relative unanimity about the available instruments and policies of reform and revolution among supporters and critics of American foreign policy is defensible. We shall find that it is not. We shall find that a better understanding of the contingent nature of international reality reveals major opportunities for the creation of a new world politics—a world politics in which force no longer plays a dominant role.

On International Reality

Although all can agree upon a catalog of international political developments, no widespread agreement exists on how to describe the fundamental features of international reality, either at this time or over time. There can be agreement on the claim that certain things are true of international reality: it is still strongly bipolar (with many states clustering around the two poles, the United States and the Soviet Union) but shows important signs of increasing multipolarity (with the emergence of a stronger Western Europe and the People's Republic of China); it has a very high degree of violence, especially if threats of use of force are viewed as violence; there is a high incidence of conflict between obvious adversaries (e.g., the United States and the Soviet Union, the Soviet Union and the Chinese People's Republic) and also among the superpowers and the underdeveloped small states. What is not clear, unfortunately, is the significance of these descriptive features of our international environment—both now and, especially, over time.

The basic reason for this uncertainty is, of course, our lack of a generally accepted, comprehensive theory of international politics that would, by its propositions, tell us what is significant. Such a theory could help us in two basic ways.

First, we have certain special concerns at the present, such as the threat of war, the desperate need for development of the underprivileged and increasingly restive and threatening states, the possible uses and the misuses of the seas and their resources, and the opportunities for tourist, business, and other intercourse with widely varying states. Our theory would enable us to see which features of the world are relevant to the occurrence or impedance of these happenings, and hence would suggest or imply guidelines for national action, especially cooperative action when interests are shared (as in prevention of major war).

Further, were the theory fully satisfactory, it would account for and thus enable us to predict significant fundamental transformations in the structure of the international system and hence in the pattern of international relations. It would therefore enable us to know in advance what basic changes could be expected and how to make the most of our expectations by preparing for those most difficult to avoid and by attempting to shape those where some discretion seemed inherent in the developing situation.

One might expect the same factors that would account for war, conflict, and development at a particular time to account also for significant changes in the nature of international relations over a long run, but this need not be the case. Indeed, it might be that the contrary would hold. For what is most significant about international relations from day to day and year to year is that they are composites of decisions made by individuals facing largely predetermined environmental situations and relying basically on tried and known policies and devices. Thus, in these short-run terms, to the policy maker there rarely seems much choice, beyond the selection of one weapon or another to pursue an end seemingly defined by the situation. In the long run, we can at least imagine significant transformations, and can often postulate basic changes that would be required to bring them about. What we generally have trouble doing is convincing the skeptical that the small day-to-day changes we envision can actually contribute to a significant long-run change in the nature of relations and hence of international reality. But what is clearest about such small changes is that they must be cumulative and synergistic (producing a whole different from and probably greater than the apparent sum of its parts) if such a transformation is to occur. And the principle of synergy is not yet widely accepted by policy makers except in the negative sense; that is, they generally expect that a situation left alone or unmet over time will expand exponentially to create a much more gigantic problem. The "Munich psychosis" and the "domino theory" are exemplary products of these views.

Put another way, we can say much that is widely recognized as significant about the conduct of relations from day to day and situation to situation. Everyone thinks these matters are subject to analysis and recommendation. But they are matters also believed to be relatively immutable—beyond our capacity to change fundamentally. In other words, the conventional wisdom about the recommendation of foreign policy holds that all that can be done is to make small momentary recommendations of an incremental sort, and the best that can be expected is incremental change. This in spite of the fact that international relations in the thirty-odd years since the outbreak of the Second World War have changed drastically several times despite—or, in another sense, perhaps because of—this conventional view about the impossibility of significant reform.

This formulation does not, however, do justice to the view. For the point is not that there cannot be significant transformations in international relations. Changes such as American opposition to Nazi Germany and concomitant alliance with the Soviet Union, followed by alliance with postwar West Germany against the Soviet Union, are perfectly acceptable and indeed even engineerable. Increasingly, scholars are coming to hold the view that this particular postwar transformation (matched by another one in Asia involving China and Japan) was, if not engineered, then at least fostered by the views and actions of American policy makers who were conscious of what was happening and of the role their views were playing in the transformation.

Rather, the conventional argument is that the only transformations that can take place are those involving alignments and stakes—never those involving the nature of relations, the kind of relations that take place between friends and between adversaries. This is why the innovations of de Gaulle were so wildly opposed in the United States and Great Britain. For de Gaulle sought to remain the ally in ultimate terms, preserving the same strong capitalist economy and authoritarian democratic political system as his major ally, the United States, but loosening the bonds so that he could be openly critical of those policies of his allies that seemed to him designed or functioning to prohibit significant fundamental transformation in the nature of relations among states. Similarly, the Soviet Union opposed outright the innovations of Tito's Yugoslavia, Nagy's short-lived Hungary, and "Prague Spring" Czechoslovakia.

It is unlikely that the purveyors of foreign policy wisdom in each major state are fully conscious of their preclusive roles —if only because they are so hostile to the notion that fundamental transformation can be brought about that they probably do not consider their attitudes and actions the fundamental barrier to it. Nonetheless, if it is not certain, it is at least plausible enough to merit the most serious and extensive consideration: the possibility that fundamental transformation of the nature of international relations might be engineered by a carefully designed and venturesomely executed foreign policy composed not of panaceas and drastic changes but of alterations in the assumptions on which our policies are grounded and hence alterations in those policies themselves. But we cannot successfully undertake development of such an alternative image of international political exigencies and opportunities without first examining the views of international reality that have undergirded the analyses of policy makers and their critics over the years. The disputes over policy and politics have often been characterized as a Great Debate—usually a debate between self-proclaimed "Idealists" and "Realists." But has this "Great Debate" increased our understanding of the nature of international reality and the opportunities for a more constructive American foreign policy?

chapter two
The Irrelevance of the Great Debate

Although there have occasionally been long and bitter debates over particular policies among policy makers and their critics, and among the scholars who have studied and criticized their behavior, there has always been fundamental agreement in the United States about the nature of international reality and the constraints that reality placed upon the free exercise of America's will in international politics.

The American Consensus

The Founding Fathers were generally agreed that the United States should retire from the affairs of Europe if European states would let the United States and its neighbors to the south alone. The argument against "entangling alliances" was not, however, as is sometimes suggested, an argument for isolation as we generally conceive it, entailing a refusal to be concerned about developments abroad and stemming from a belief that such affairs are without significance for the basic interests of the United States. Rather, the argument was based on a widespread belief that the United States had an important "civilizing mission" to play for the traditional colonialist nations of Europe—the role of convincing these states that they should reform their internal politics to accord more individual freedom and opportunities for economic initiative to their citizens, and that they should learn to live at peace with themselves and others. Nevertheless, those holding this view realized that such recommendations were foreign to the elites of the European states, and would remain unimpressive to them until there was a prospering and attention-getting example of the success of such policies. The Fathers decided that the United States should be that moral example, and they set about toward that end by refraining from involvement in quarrels they believed temporary and ultimately insignificant, while concentrating their efforts on the internal development of the United States.

Seen from this commencement, the emergence of the United States into major political relations with the states of Europe at the close of the nineteenth century—in the Spanish-American War and then ultimately in the First World War—is much less of a change in policy than it is a change in the calculation of the American leadership about the readiness of the United States to make its splendid development and moral example better known and something to be reckoned with.

The "Great Debate"

It has often been argued—by scholars and politicos—that Woodrow Wilson's efforts, once the United States had become involved in the First World War, to shape the peace to be constructed thereafter was a policy so "idealistic" (as the term goes) that it was doomed to failure. Many pictures of Wilson's views of world politics as well as of his negotiation with the European leaders at Versailles suggest that his expressed hope that nations would thereupon begin to live at peace with one another and resolve their disputes through resort to international law and arbitration was based on a mistaken assessment of the importance of force in shaping the behavior of states in their world. However Wilson's ideas have been construed, careful study of his foreign policy,

let alone his pronouncements both at Versailles and subsequently in the United States as he sought political ratification
of the Treaty and America's entry into the League of Nations,
shows conclusively that his contention was that nations
should be offered the opportunity to observe international
law, and if they did not do so they should be compelled to do
so through the application of military force, whether by the
League of Nations or by individual nations. Moreover, he
stated time and again that it should be made clear to such
states in advance of their decisions that force impended if they
refused to behave civilly (as he conceived civility). And his
policy in Latin America foreshadowed that toward the rest of
the world. Thus his foreign policy is really in its moral fervor
a continuation of the policy of the Founding Fathers, and in
its promise of American power at the service of rectitude a
statement that the country had finally reached a posture of
power that it had not had earlier and that it would employ in
the fashion subsequently to be advocated by all American
secretaries of state and presidents since the Second World
War.

Prior to American involvement in the First World War,
there had been a growing movement to encourage all states to
adhere to agreements calling for compulsory binding arbitration in the event of international disputes—a movement near
to the heart of William Howard Taft. But even this movement,
and Taft- himself, stated quite clearly that the alternative to
such agreement was military self-help, and where feasible,
compulsion of the derelicts to behave better than they were
otherwise inclined.

The same should be said for the efforts after the First
World War to achieve disarmament. They were designed for
naval disarmament rather than comprehensive disarmament,
and the propositions entertained and briefly subscribed to
were intended more to save resources from needless expendi-

ture in a realm subject to rapid obsolescence than they were to create an international climate of trust and cooperation.

These years between the world wars are generally viewed as the years of "Idealism" (as the Wilsonian approach to international politics has been somewhat misleadingly termed) in power. They saw, however, but one effort at altering international relations that seemed at its inception to be a fundamental departure from international politics as usual. This was the proposal that became the Kellogg-Briand Pact and called upon each state to renounce resort to war as an instrument of national policy. When the major states assembled to subscribe to the document in Paris in 1928, however, they produced a statement with little consciousness of the nature of international relations; and when the various states ratified it, each added its own favorite reservations, so that ultimately what the states had done was agree not to wage war unless they determined that war was necessary to the attainment or maintenance of their national interests.

Nonetheless, some progress was made in reshaping international relations in accordance with the expressed hopes and visions of the Idealists—the emphases on observance of international law, resort to binding arbitration when disputes arose, disarming to ease tensions and make war less prosecutable, cooperating in the enforcement of the peace through the actions of the League of Nations, and the subscription to statements renouncing the resort to war. But these measures failed to alter international relations significantly, and meanwhile other forces were at play, undermining the position of those conducting the foreign policy of America.

The rise and military activity of Hitler's Germany, when coupled with the failure of the states of Western Europe and the United States itself to foresee and prevent its military rapacity, led to a discrediting of the Idealists. Their difficulties were not, in fact, primarily a failure to appreciate the impor-

tance of military force in international politics—as their Realist subsequents were continually to claim—so much as an
inability to get their minds and resources allocated to international adventure at a time of continuing national privation
and depression. The "Realists" (as they preferred to term
themselves) had little to say about the importance and indeed
the desirability of a strong national posture and a willingness
to employ military force that the Idealists had not said all
along. The chief difference—more pronounced among the
scholars than among the statesmen until the years of the cold
war—was the Realists' abandonment of the pious hopes and
utopian speculations that generally characterized Idealist rhetoric. For where the Idealists had generally emphasized the
finer world that might be anticipated if only the state remained strong and exercised its power firmly but judiciously,
the Realists came close to claiming that the development and
employment of military force was essential to the present survival of the state, and that effective employment of force
might ultimately educate the adversary to behave more civilly
at some point in the (perhaps distant) future.

    It would not be accurate to conclude, then, that no differ-
ences existed between the Idealists and the Realists. But it
would be wrong to believe that the Idealists were opposed to
the exercise of military force to influence, and where possible
to control, the behavior of other states. The Idealists were
actually in accord with the Realists on this matter. They were,
however, somewhat more optimistic about the promise of such
a strategy in reordering the world and reforming the states,
and hence their utopias were supposed to be more imminent.
One other difference followed from this and was most clearly
evident in the pronouncements of President Dwight D. Eisenhower's Secretary of State, John Foster Dulles. The Idealists
had exercised their moralism primarily in announcing their
continuing refusal to be drawn into the ugly conduct of their

cohorts abroad and in designing their utopias, while the Realists—who could no more renounce moralism than their predecessor Idealists—converted their moralism into a combination of righteous indignation and certainty of the rectitude of
their posture—displaying, thereby, a lack of what the Founding Fathers had referred to as "a decent respect for the opin-
ions of Mankind." They became, in other words, contemptu-
ous not only of their predecessor Idealists, whom they deemed
weak as well as unrealistic, but also of those in other states
who differed with them about the rectitude of American policy or who emphasized their hopes that the tenor of international relations would improve significantly with the advent
of the nuclear age and their beliefs that it was the primary
responsibility of the greatest power on earth, the United
States, to play a major role in that improvement by refraining
from predatory behavior and bullying. For the Realists generally conceived of America's responsibility, on the contrary, as
educating their inferiors around the globe about the appropriate rules for the exercise of power in the service of the Realist
conception of international peace and harmony.

Thus the expectable efforts after the Second World War
to reconstruct an international order that promised greater
stability and peaceful progress turned into efforts to ensure
the newly expanded American presence and influence around
the globe. The emphasis was placed upon stability or continuity at the expense of progress. Thus the United Nations was
viewed as a possible vehicle by which the United States and
its friends could defeat the Soviet Union and its friends, not
just in the frequent voting in the Security Council and the
General Assembly, but also in Korea, where UN sanction was
sought and gained for the American "police action" in fighting
to restore the status quo ante. And suggestions and discussions of disarmament were transmogrified into technical considerations of highly limited measures of arms control. The

Soviet Union, meanwhile, in its own conceived "sphere of influence," was behaving in a way that complemented America's self-assertion. The behavior of each reinforced that of the other. And thus was born and bred the cold war.

At this early point in our analysis it is neither possible nor desirable to attempt to allocate blame between the major powers for the failure to succeed in reconstructing international relations on a basis less violent and more productive of welfare. What is important to understand is the intellectual basis for policy—adopted and implemented in similar degree by both the United States and the Soviet Union—by which the old patterns of international relations were perpetuated.

The core of the theoretical assumptions about international politics made by policy makers in the United States (and, it would appear, in the Soviet Union as well) in the years since 1945 has been derived from the Realist analysis of international politics. This analysis has begun with an assumption (an assumption that is "factual" in the sense that it is subject to testing by evidence accessible to all) that the adversary is single-mindedly and all-resourcefully hostile to us and our system, and hence can be expected to do whatever he can to combat, weaken, and destroy our system wherever it exists and replace it with his own whenever possible.

The Realist analysis has then added a "theoretical" assumption—that is, an assumption about how to operate in the world, grounded in beliefs about the causal mechanisms or principles at work in the world. This assumption, crudely put, is that the way to deal effectively with an adversary—or at least with an adversary as conceived by the Realist analysis— is with force, both potential or threatened and actual or employed, or at least with a skillful combination of force and an offer of conciliation should the interests and actions of the adversary change. The implicit argument of this reasoning was, of course, that this sort of posture and action by the

United States would not only protect the United States but also, through the principle of "operant conditioning" (in which approved behavior is strengthened by reward and disapproved behavior is extinguished by punishment), educate or train the Soviet Union to change its behavior so that we could then afford to change ours; and eventually there would result an improvement in the nature of international relations.

Explanation of why policy makers and analysts—most of whom have agreed with this reasoning—settled upon this reliance on force to bring about the education of a misguided adversary is beyond the scope of this essay. But several considerations are relevant. The first is the obvious impact of the coming of World War II in "disproving" the alternative Idealist paradigm or theory, which had generally suggested that all nations could be rationally persuaded to agree to accept binding universal arbitration, to establish an effective international peace-keeping organization, to abide by further developed international law, to undertake general and complete disarmament, or to settle upon some combination of these.

Furthermore, the resort to force had its effective place in previous times in the service of two objectives: repression by vested interests (such as was pronounced in the feudal era, in which it was acceptable because convention bound all relations and protected the individual while rewarding the risk-taking nobility with expansion of its interests); and revolution by the oppressed (such as had its rise in the religious wars and their sequels that were then the effective and only way one set of interests could replace another set). Both of these historical stages in the resort to force, the repression by vested interests and the revolution by the oppressed, used force in a strictly instrumental fashion: force promised attainment of the objective sought (and indeed allowed it); and other conditions were propitious or at least allowed success to the skillful and imaginative. Today, this forceful resort remains in favor but conditions have changed radically—due primarily to changes in the technologies of energy (for destruction) and transportation coupled with information gathering and processing, and to the proliferation of nation-states and accompanying nationalism that has fractured the world and created multitudes of potential battlegrounds. Thus there now seems to be a fundamental impossibility to the satisfactory resort to force that did not hold when force was effectively employed to maintain or alter the status quo.

The actual impact of this continuing resort to force in our postwar years, as any who observe international politics can clearly see, has been the expectable consequences of militarization: violence, death, misery, and lack of freedom for many of the world's citizenry. The effect on political interaction itself has been primarily stagnation and deterioration, caused by the fact that force has generally been met with force and little has changed. There are, of course, those who would count this a significant gain, because they greet with equanimity and even joy the maintenance of an approximate status quo territorially and are not impressed by the loss of life, liberty, and welfare or their promise as much as others are.

The indictment implicit in this analysis is, of course, applicable to both the superpowers and to the major powers below them as well. No state emerges from the cold war years with an impressive record in any terms except those of maintaining its own specially vested territorial and economic interests at great cost not only to other peoples but to its own citizens as well.

There was a time, before the proliferation of new states and the expansion of political mobilization, when such achievements were viewed as not only desirable but also praiseworthy and promising of greater stability in the future. Indeed, that presumption, we have argued, underlies the Realist conception of the most promising approach to peace. But given the strong feelings of both major adversaries and increasingly their clients that their systems are fundamentally incompatible, the presumption results not in stability and peace so much as in arms races, military escalation in armed conflict situations, and generalized political conflict that could end only if one side gives up (as neither seems willing or even able to do) or if there is a drastic shift in the patterns of interaction between adversaries. Some have, in the past, held out hope that the two major adversaries would learn to live with each other through establishment of the principle of "peaceful coexistence" (in large part a modern version of the increasingly ineffective doctrine of "spheres of influence"). But the emergence of the People's Republic of China, and reactions to it by the major powers, indicate that this would at best be a stopgap measure and that if any significant decrease in the violence content of international relations is to be achieved it will require major alteration in the patterns of conflict.

Thus, neither the critics arguing for world government on one extreme nor those arguing for preventive war on the other have promised the effective transit from our present to their proffered future without unacceptable risk. The reason for this is clear—or at least the unacceptability of the various existing proposals is clear. World-government advocates have called for a new moral and self-sacrificial national departure coupled with the same by all other states, but they have not been able to come to terms with the question of how this instantaneous change can be engendered and implemented with drastic precision and coordination, for they have thought that one could simply be concerned with the policies and actions of each state individually rather than with the established and continually changeable pattern of multinational interaction. If their efforts had focused on this interaction they might have been able to devise a route to this objective that promised attainment if only all could be brought to agree on the desirability of the objective. But if there was a time when all might have so agreed (and that is at least doubtful), that time seems clearly past now. For the most significant trends today are toward the development of attitudes that are anti-state on the surface (the state is tyrannical and inefficient because it is bureaucratic and hence removed from the concerns and the control of its citizens) but would be even more anti-"world-state" than they are anti-"nation-state," since a world-state would be even more remote than a nation-state and would not have the compensatory advantage of popular nationalism to induce and retain popular support.

But if changes in the technology and software of rule have made propositions of world government increasingly unacceptable, developments in military technology have rendered arguments for preventive war even more so, for they have guaranteed that the preventer would be destroyed by automatic retaliation from the state he has attacked.

Virtually all analysts and policy makers have seen these twin developments. And thus there has been a renewed search for an acceptable alternative to Idealism and Realism.

The Neorealist Critique

Increasingly in recent years the long-standing Realist position has been subject to criticism, not merely from a few residual optimistic Idealists, but also from a growing group that might be termed "Neorealists." The primary factor in the rise of this amorphous group was the abject failure of the Realist approach to Southeast Asia and especially Vietnam. As Vietnam became more depressing and less promising of eventual success even to the outright Realists who controlled American policy, the domestic situation in the United States deteriorated drastically, both because of outright opposition to the Vietnam adventure by a growing coalition of peace advocates and the student Left, and especially because of the surge of black radicalism and lesser strains of racial agitation. This domestic development, increasingly salient because of major peace demonstrations and periodic riots and other racial disturbances in major cities, apparently led a number of previous supporters of the Realist policy abroad to reconsider their own ordering of American resource allocation priorities. It also, very importantly, provided a convenient opportunity for those basically opposed to American adventurism to appeal their case to the people. Thus there grew increasing suggestion that our attention should be given in greater measure to the fundamental domestic problems, especially those of prejudice and poverty—and from that point people increasingly recognized the expense of dealing with the multitude of pollutions to which all people in industrial and even many pastoral areas are more and more subject.

What emerged from this disparate enlightenment was, of course, increasing claim that if we did reexamine our priorities we would find that the first and most important claim on our limited national resources was domestic. Thus, we must find a way of lessening our expansive involvement overseas to free scarce resources for domestic concerns.

This argument merits considerable attention, not for its truth, but for the revelation it is of the simple-mindedness of much analysis of the capabilities and difficulties of the United States. It is certainly not true literally that our national resources are so limited that we cannot be both venturesome abroad and constructive at home. Our world wartime mobilization of resources has several times proved that. What is true, however, is that our politicians are generally unwilling to call for the kind of minor sacrifice that would be required to do this while the major unusual drain on our resources is a war that is unpopular with many of the people. Thus it has become convenient for increasing numbers of national politicians as well as occasional renegade academic Realists to call for a reallocation of attention and resources to the domestic needs of the country.

The great misfortune of this call is that is has enabled the Realists to escape with their theory relatively unscathed. What might have proved a crucial test of the validity of the Realist argument that the employment of military forces wherever we choose can be effective in influencing the flow of events, has instead generally resulted primarily in this call for a reallocation of resources based primarily on the urgent new priority, and secondarily on a discovery that effective foreign intervention is more costly and more difficult than the Realists had claimed. But, very unfortunately, this shift in emphasis is exactly that, rather than a learning of the lesson of failure of our adventurism, and of the Realist analysis underlying it.

And the unfortunate result of this will probably be that we will, in shifting our resources to domestic matters, ignore not only this lesson that should be learned about the inefficacy of interventionist military force in the Third World, but even more, the fact that military force itself, employed as the Realists have long proposed and demonstrated, has not and will not—indeed, cannot—bring about the significant improvement in the relations among nations that all of us desire. In other words, the resort to the argument about scarce resources and new priorities is preventing us both from learning fully the lessons of Vietnam and from actively seeking new ways of engineering the improvement in international relations that is so crucial to the survival of most of what we value at home and abroad.

These circumstances, then, are allowing the Neorealists and their forebears to continue to accept the inevitability of violence and "illfare" when nations interact, but to believe that a great state need not necessarily interact all around the world all the time, and hence to recommend that the United States cut its commitments and thereby, in ignoring festering sores elsewhere, decrease the violence content in the world.

These Neorealists, who argue in general for cutting commitments but then pursuing approximately the same foreign policy on a smaller scale, are liable to several debilitating criticisms. First, most of the commitment cutting they recommend will serve at best only to postpone facing problems, especially because their view of what the United States ultimately seeks in the world and how it must ultimately attempt to achieve and maintain its vital interests is in harmony with traditional Realist prescriptions. The chief difficulty here is that their analysis ignores the bases for our involvement around the world. And unless those bases are ultimately only the pleasures of past involvement recollected in tranquility, those bases will continue to assert themselves and gradually suck the United States back into far-flung involvements—whether those bases prove to be American economic interests, the military influence on American policy, the beliefs about our responsibilities held by American leaders, the generous inclinations and concerns of the American people, the attraction of occasional popular distraction from intractable painful domestic problems (increasingly tempting, perhaps, as we come to realize our utter inability to solve our crushing urban problems), or even the character of an international political system rent by turmoil and including some states out for self-aggrandizement.

These factors combine in complex ways to provide the occasions and impetus for American involvement with the rest of the world. They do not disappear when the United States lowers its profile, pulls in its sails, lessens commitments, encourages self-reliance, or otherwise removes itself from international politics. Indeed, if our withdrawal has any effect on them, it is likely to strengthen many of them. And thus a "neoisolationism" or even simply, as some would characterize it, a "neorealism" seems to hold no promise of anything but a respite—and perhaps a costly one—in America's active involvement in world affairs.

For these various but quite similar prescriptions for what is usually termed a "more realistic" foreign policy for the United States (and, one can imagine, for the Soviet Union as well, following its setbacks in Cuba, Indonesia, and Eastern Europe, and its vicious conflict with the Chinese People's Republic)—these prescriptions too fail to understand the nature of international reality sufficiently to be able to recommend a course of action that promises anything but a resumption of the same reciprocally interventionist military involvement around the world. Nothing in the recommendations of the Hans Morgenthaus, the William Fulbrights, the Richard Nixons, the Eugene McCarthys, and all their political and intellectual kith and kin offers any way of avoiding an expansion of involvements to a renewed globalism—especially if we should seem to succeed at mastering the smaller but still substantial slice of the globe to which they all recommend devotion of our attention and resources. And, perhaps much more significantly, nothing in their recommendations promises any significant alteration in the balance between military and non-military activities and resources devoted to the pursuit of our sliced-down interests. In other, and harsh but accurate, words, the whole contemporary Neorealist school of foreign policy recommendation simply calls for more of the same policies in less of the same places. But if these policies did not work effectively, either to contain communism or other nationalist movements in much of the Third World or to bring about development in those same countries, either to reopen Eastern Europe to Western democratic ways or to foster significant integration in Western Europe—if these policies failed where they were most concertedly directed previously, in a period in which they were designed—what reason is there to believe that they will succeed now if we but cut back on the extent of our involvements?

There is no more reason to believe in the likely success

of these policies today and tomorrow internationally than there is to believe that the New Deal welfare programs and the subsequent civil rights legislation will satisfactorily solve our drastic urban problems. But, unfortunately, while many are recognizing the inadequacy of the old approaches to our domestic problems and are finally seeking to develop drastically new means for coping with them, the same is not true of our foreign policy and the international problems of violence and servitude and almost universal impoverishment it is supposed to solve.

Is There an Alternative?

The Neorealist argument is little more than a dilution of the Realist argument. This has been one of its great appeals to most of its advocates: it does not require a fundamental rethinking of the nature of international conflict and the promising means of coping with that conflict in defense of what the Realists term "the national interest." Rather, of course, the Neorealist argument is that we should simply do less of the same thing internationally. The attractions of such a proposal, at a time when the Realist approach that has shaped American foreign policy at least since 1945 is in so much difficulty, are immense. And so are its dangers.

Thus we desperately need an alternative to the Neorealism that seems already to be dominating public debate and private policy making. But what might that alternative be? It is certainly not immediately obvious. We have difficulty conceiving of a real alternative, partly because the task is so great, and partly because the discussion of international politics and policy has always been conducted essentially in terms and concepts developed by and for the conventional wisdom of Idealism, Realism, and Neorealism.

But it seems appropriate now to assume that, because the old approaches have failed so drastically, novel approaches are in order, or at least are worth development and examination. The challenge, then, is for creativity in the analysis of the underlying bases of the problems and the nature of the international reality within which they are fostered or fester, and then for innovation in insinuating new approaches into the inevitably ongoing process of international relations. It may be hoped that an adequate understanding of the nature of that dynamic international reality, while it will not in itself offer solutions to the problems arising within component units of the international system, will enable us to understand better the crucial context within which those solutions must succeed, and will further offer us possibilities for their implementation and fostering. But such innovation must be based on a much more profound understanding of international reality as a process of interactive dependence, as well as a much more creative development of policies to cope with the problems of violence, poverty, and servitude. A promising improvement in America's role in international affairs, if it is possible at all, will require not withdrawal but active participation. But if that participation is to contribute to an improvement in international relations, it must be based upon a deeper and different understanding of international political processes, and the development of a new constructive role that America might play in international relations.

chapter three
The Crucial
Contribution of
American Foreign Policy

The most debilitating problem facing a reformist state in international relations is that all it has to work with essentially is its own foreign policy, coupled at times with the fragile and incomplete structure of international law and an occasional weak international organization. Although most reformist actions depend for their success upon major changes in the actions of other states (whether those actions be joining a federation or letting neighbors live in peace), the focus of recommendations by a reformist must ultimately be the foreign policy of a given state. And for our reformist interests, our focus must be the foreign policy of the United States. Thus the question is, What can the United States, equipped primarily with its foreign policy, do to alter international relations constructively?

Traditionally, the answer—especially by the self-pronounced Realists but also by other species of pessimist—has been that the United States can do little or nothing to alter the nature of international reality—a reality, we are continually reminded, significantly characterized by conflict among would-be sovereign states in a world of scarce material resources and prestige. This reality, it is continually argued, sets such bounds upon the action of any single participant, or even upon a concert of major participants, that little or nothing can be done to alter the nature of interaction beyond changing the distribution of the scarce resources both material and prestigial. If the analyst or the recommender accepts this argument, there is little he can propose beyond small meliorist measures —most of which must take the form of recommendations of greater benevolence or further withdrawal from the conflict, and hence from international relations. And our past efforts at withdrawal (as present advocates of reduced commitment and participation are tirelessly reminded) have not been productive of greater international peace and welfare.

Seeing the hopelessness of coping with the Realists on their own terms, most recommenders have either accepted the Realist analysis of international reality and used it as a basis for recommendation of withdrawal (Fortress America or inward-turned America) or have chosen to postulate a drastically different Idealist Reality in which states and their men are basically good rather than evil, generous rather than selfish, and would cooperate rather than conflict if only they were given the chance. These premises are so at odds with manifest behavior, both at home and abroad, that they must be accepted on faith or not at all. And unfortunately, even if they are accepted on faith, the way to alter behavior so that it corresponds with nature—or the way to allow this deeper reality to manifest itself—has never been prescribed in a way convincing to either academic Realists or policy makers.

Most of the hundreds of analysts and publicists who have written books on American foreign policy in the years since 1945 have also asked and answered the question of what America can do. But if the answers they have given are taken as definitive (if somewhat contradictory), the preponderant conclusion must be that the United States cannot do much beyond simply being better informed and more efficient, except perhaps for curtailing its involvement in international affairs. And there is scarcely much agreement that such curtailment would be worthwhile. For many analysts fear that isolationism, neoisolationism, or shrinkage of our "sphere of interest" would necessarily prove to be a short-lived and treacherous policy: it would result in rapid deterioration of our position and our expectable fate in the world—as did isolation in the years between the world wars—and would then force us to return to the fray from a position much weakened by the gains of our adversaries during our self-imposed constraint.

It is possible to devise schemes for such curtailment that seem not to threaten serious deterioration of our position in the world—at least, given what seem to be defensible presumptions about the direction of world politics in most parts of the world today. Still, such proposals suffer primarily, in terms of our objectives, from a lack of constructive impact. They seem to offer less pain and less cost to us, simply because we will not be in the fray and hence cannot lose or win costly victories. But they do not, and indeed they cannot, really offer hope of reform of international politics in general. The reason for this is simple.

The approach of our nation's Founding Fathers and their offspring—that the way to reform the actions of others was to set a moral example at some distance—did not work then, and there seems no reason to believe that it would work better now. The nations that have some chance of influencing the attitudes and actions of other states are the nations that are actively involved in the affairs of states, setting positive examples of constructive or destructive behavior in their relations with others. Thus the aloof nation may be appreciated by those states in whose affairs it does not meddle abusively, but it will almost certainly not be emulated. And so the question is, What sort of policy can the United States adopt that will offer a positive example to others, will itself contribute to the reconstruction of world politics, and will at the same time minimize the risk of disaster to the United States while contributing to the attainment of our essential immediate interests?

No promising answer to this question is obvious. And so this would seem a rather hopeless situation. The Realists and Neorealists not only have control of policy, but also have impressive apparent evidence of the accuracy of their world view in the nature of international relations which we find so abhorrent. There seems to be no drastically different policy that promises significant success, given this obviously dominant reality, and there seems no promising transformation strategy either, for the gap between the proposed transformations and reality as we know it seems so wide that it cannot be bridged by less than an act of God.

Were this appearance true, the recommendations of the Realists, and of virtually all our policy makers, that we reconcile ourselves to our situation and simply do the best we can under admittedly unpropitious circumstances for now and into the indefinite (but quite clearly distant) future, would seem impeccable (if, in candor, appalling). If there really is a reality so recalcitrant as that painted by the Realist analysts and theorists, what indeed is the room for maneuver, let alone the promise for reform or revolution?

But this argument from reality has a fatal flaw. And it is time we recognized and exploited it. The argument itself manifests a fundamental misunderstanding of the nature of reality over time. It is based on a fundamental misunderstanding of the role of the United States in the creation and maintenance of international reality. This is not to say, as transformational theorists have in the past, that a drastic change in American foreign policy alone would thereupon reform that reality. It would not. It would probably instead destroy the United

States as an actor in international politics—and perhaps as an entity. On this much the Realist analysis of international reality is correct. No system in the history of relations among would-be sovereign states in a world of great scarcity has ever been transformable in such a fashion. But neither has reality ever been as immutable as the Realists have argued that it has always been. To understand the limits of possible transformation, and hence to be able to recommend a foreign policy for the United States that promises to engineer or contribute drastically to the alteration of reality as we know and lament it, we must first examine, not so much the nature of the reality we face as the process of reality creation.

PART TWO

The Essentials
of a New American
Understanding

chapter four

The Continuous Creation
of International Reality

The reconstruction of alliances since the Second World War, the development in weaponry that obsesses the thoughts and pervades the policies of most states, the rise of the Third World to independence and often intervention-enticing conflict, along with scores of other developments, make it impossible for anyone—policy maker, scholar, or attentive citizen—to believe that contemporary international relations do not change. But if there can be no disputing the fact that international relations change, there is much dispute over which changes are significant rather than superficial, as there is more basically dispute over how to distinguish the significant changes from the insignificant. And there is drastic dispute over the significance—the depth and lastingness—of even those changes that are obvious to all, let alone over the causes of those changes that are deemed significant.

Explaining Changes in International Reality

This uncertainty about the causes of basic changes is manifest in the efforts generally made to explain changes. Such explanations are often made in terms of systemic factors, such as the asserted bipolar structure of the world (with all nations affected by the polarization of the

United States and the Soviet Union) or its breakdown with the rise of a United Europe and the People's Republic of China. Or explanations are made in terms of external factors such as the development of nuclear weapons or intercontinental ballistic missiles.

More specific explanations are often made in terms of decisions by very willful major leaders, such as Truman's creation of the Marshall Plan, de Gaulle's decisions to veto British entry into the Common Market and to leave NATO, Kennedy's decision to force Khrushchev to back down in Cuba, or other actions viewed as consciously engineered turning points in history.

Even the recent efforts to complexify explanations by reference to bureaucratic infighting within a government—a consequence primarily of the ugliness of Vietnam and the unwillingness of most to claim or to admit to responsibility for such a collection of miscalculations and misadventures—have failed to resolve the uncertainty over which changes in international relations are fundamental, and what has caused them.

All of these explanations share in some crucial and generally obvious weaknesses. First, they are *not intersubjective* —they are not easily passed on from one explainer to another, let alone agreed to by both. There is considerable disagreement among the explainers, and their differences do not seem to be reconcilable. Second, and as a consequence, the explanations are generally *not cumulative*. When explanations of various events are pieced together, they do not fit well enough to give us a better understanding of any of the events, let alone of international relations in general. We do not learn more by more study.

Third, and not surprisingly, they are *not reliable*. Thus we are told of "revolution" after "revolution"—the atomic bomb, the American foreign aid program, the hydrogen bomb, the postwar military alliances, the colonial independence movement, the missile age, the era of multinational organizations, etc. Much as international relations do change, they do not change rapidly enough to allow each of these "revolutions" a significance of the sort often ascribed. In retrospect, so much of our analysis has been so bad.

Furthermore, most of the explanations of these changes have been cast in terms of apparently or assertedly *eternal verities*—about the motives of states, their fundamental interests and inclinations, and even about the importance of factors such as technology, military establishments, geography, or national honor and credibility. If the changes are as drastic as they are so often claimed to be, can there be so many eternally valid factors, and can these factors be themselves so unchanged by all these so-called revolutions? If so, has there really been the drastic and significant change that even these analysts claim to see? The difficulties here may be only conceptual and terminological. But they seem to be more the consequence of superficial and often self-contradictory explanation by "eternal verities."

If this varied collection of characteristics of so much explanation of change in international relations seems crippling or even lethal, there remain several others more important still for our purposes. Most such analyses of international relations, most explanations of the major changes of our age, are *not really understandable in human terms* nor do they offer implications relevant for those desirous of encouraging more constructive change in international relations.

We require, if we are not to give up hope and cease our efforts for a better world, explanations of the major changes of our times that show what roles people have played and must continue to play in the shaping of those relations, that show how our actions and even our thoughts have been and are shaped by both material developments *and* by unconscious assumptions we ourselves have made, and that indicate what sorts of changes are possible and promising in material factors, in assumptions, and even more in our understanding of the relations between our images of the world and the material conditions in the world. Unless our explanations of the nature and changes of international relations are consciously directed toward these considerations and formulated in terms relevant to the way in which men view and act in their world (whether these men be policy makers, scholars, or attentive citizens), our explanations will be of little relevance *even if they overcome* these other weaknesses.

To achieve this understanding with implications for constructive change will require that we know the bases of international relations—what does and what does not change, what can and what cannot change—and how crucial fundamental change can be encouraged or engineered.

Such a posture will seem hubris or folly to those convinced that either divine will or material rules man, that revolutions in international relations happen in spite of rather than because of the way we act in the world. Indeed, if we took much of our international political explanation seriously, we would have to share in this reticence and even hostility. But the fact is that while some of us explain events in terms of material conditions, most of us act in terms of a belief that what we think about the nature of the world matters immensely to what happens to our world and to us within it. And in this natural attitude lies the germ of a new way of understanding and changing international politics.

The Social Creation of International Reality

While we all simplify intellectually by assuming and asserting that there is a concrete reality "out there" that exists, continues to exist over time, and is essentially independent of "what goes on in our minds," the fact is that the crucial elements of reality—especially of social reality, the web of interrelations in which man finds himself—are socially created. Our institutions—the patterns of interactions with others by which we establish whether or not our images of reality "out there" are correct—are created by the thoughts we have and share with others.

This phenomenon, the social creation of reality, is perhaps difficult to grasp in the abstract. But it is quite clear in interpersonal relations. Love, for example the love relationship between two people (whether based in sexual drive, need for companionship, or whatever else), is created by the development and sharing of certain attitudes of desire, caring, dependence. It cannot exist as a relationship (that is, as something "out there" in "reality," which affects the behavior of both parties), unless there is a contribution of dispositions or attitudes by each party to its creation. This is not to say that each party will have the same image of "the reality of the relationship." Indeed, the biographical differences between any two people make that virtually impossible, for they ensure that there will be differences in perception, differences in comprehension, differences in expectation, and differences in action. When those differences are too great, the reality created conjointly is one of indifference, misunderstanding, or hostility. When the differences are small, when the similarities are conducive to a sharing of desire, caring, and dependence, love or a love relationship has been created—socially created. And, of course, as it has been created, so can it be destroyed.

This process is quite clear in interpersonal relations when we think of them in terms of the shared and not-shared elements of the images of reality of the several parties. Further reflection makes the process of reality creation in terms of social groups clearer, as, for example, in the largely collective (collectively generated, shared, perpetuated, and altered) images and hence relations of racial groups. We know we are "born into" and socialized and educated in terms of variously socially shared images of other racial groups (especially as they relate to our own group). We also know that we generally tend at any one time to believe that these images reflect "reality" (whether they be that "Negroes are dirty" or that "Blacks are sexually superior to whites" or whatever). These images are subject to change with conditioning but—and this is most important—while the images persist they not only tend to perpetuate themselves in the minds of men, but also tend to alter reality itself in various, often complex and sometimes unanticipated, ways. Thus the belief that "Negroes are dirty" may lead whites to be more conscious of dirty collars on blacks and less conscious of dirty collars on whites (thereby tending to confirm the "truth" of the stereotype in the minds of whites semi-consciously) while it may lead blacks to be overly careful. In any event, while the image persists it will further interfere with human relations between the races. The notion that "Blacks are sexually superior to whites," apparently more widely believed in America now than the image of dirtiness, is even more interesting to analyze in terms of its varying impacts upon, not merely the beliefs, but the actions and hence the evidence against which such beliefs are occasionally checked.

But we need not engage in any further analysis to see the point it demonstrates: the role that socially shared images of reality play in influencing that reality over time, even when it is large social groups rather than just several individuals that are involved.

The basic point—that our assumptions about the nature and especially the fundamental constraints of reality shape that reality—is true of politics within states and other smaller units, and also true of the economy and society at large. But it is considerably more true of international politics than it is in many other areas. The reason for this greater impact on international politics is not immediately obvious, for we tend to assume that because international politics is a quite aggregate phenomenon it is far removed from individual influence.

International politics always has been the province of a very small percentage of the world's people, especially when it was under the direct and highly undemocratic control of the foreign office, the diplomatic corps, and other elitist and generally unaccessible (for either participation or influence by regular people) social groups. At that time, the only impact of the masses was in their service in the armed forces—something the elite was slow to appreciate, let alone require. The coming of the citizen armies might then be thought to tend to reverse this trend by adding a major social group to the decision; but as we know, those conscripted have never been allowed, let alone encouraged, to play a role in developing policy (although their attitudes and actions have certainly affected outcomes), and the closest they have generally come (at least until the Vietnam war) to making assumptions about international reality has been accepting the general line that their participation is necessary to preserve or reestablish peace and equilibrium in international relations in the interest of their state.

But as this citizen participation increased, there have been further developments that have probably intensified the opportunities for policy makers' assumptions to shape reality. For as armies have increased in size and capability for destruction, the acceptability of actual fighting (employing that massive destructive capacity) has been increasingly seen as lessening, and thus international relations have been increasingly transformed into a continuing interplay of deterrence strategies. Nothing could more conclusively embody our contention about reality creation than the deterrence theorizing and posturing that are now so pervasive. As deterrence theorists are so fond of pointing out, it is not the actual threat but the believed threat, not the actual capability but the believed capability, that matters in determining international political outcomes—so long as nations do not move to actual combat. Further, this is by no means a feature of international relations exploited only in the interests of military objectives and military dominance. Most deterrence theorists fancy themselves prescribing ways to successful maintenance of the peace. Thus, at least if we are willing to make some charitable assumptions about the ethical goodness of our theorists, we can view their words as not only tending to confirm our contention, but also showing how such postulations about the adversary and what affects him can be put in the service of improving the quality of international relations.

This is not to say that material factors play no real role, or set no important limits to the malleability of international politics. For it is quite clear that in times previous to our highly developed technologies of transport, destruction, and information processing, geography was a major constraint upon international political activity—as it remains to varying extents for less developed and less wealthy states. Similarly, economic constraints first limited technological development and now, through their determination of relative costs when coupled with preferences, affect the desirability and immediate possibility of much foreign action. And again, these economic considerations remain of considerable constraint to the less developed and less endowed states today.

But it is important to see the continuing (and perhaps even increasing) role that mental images and assumptions play in determining the nature and extent of even these material constraints. Thus, for example, it is mentally established preferences that are the greatest determinant of economic cost through their creation of differential demand and their longer-run determination of available supply, and further of technological development, in that they provide goals and beliefs about what will be possible and economically feasible in terms of technological development and proliferation. If the point is unclear, we need only consider the unparalleled and unanticipated extent of American economic development through its history, which has resulted from mentally generated desires coupled with action that seemed to assume it possible contrary to conventional wisdom, or the stupendous achievements in space that were again achieved primarily because decision makers assumed the achievements would be possible and decided to pay the costs their attainment would incur.

A prime source of difficulty or misunderstanding in our concept of "reality" seems to be our understandable tendency in thinking of reality to center first on material factors or conditions that are indeed virtually immutable. Geographic position is perhaps the best example of this, although climate would also be appropriate. Nonetheless, if we ruminate on geographical position we will see that, while it cannot be actually changed (barring national expansion or an imperial policy, of course), it can be virtually eliminated as a constraint through the application of technology—as the major powers have done militarily through application of the technologies of transportation, communication, and destruction to their military development. And this suggests what seems an important qualification: material elements of reality are probably best viewed as alterable over the long run rather than as eternally and completely constraining.

Nonetheless, there can be no doubt that such long-term alterable material elements of reality are serious constraints. Among the most important are available natural resources and the personal attributes—motivations and skills—of the populace. These two factors together combine as the major determinants of the general state of the economy, which in itself may be viewed as a material element of reality that is generally constraining and alterable only over the long term.

But the economy might also be placed in a third and significantly different category, among those aspects of reality that are highly interactively dependent. For it is clear today (as it might also have been earlier but was not) that the economic status of a nation is most heavily dependent upon the economic status of many other nations as and because they interact so widely and necessarily. The lessons of the reparations policy following the First World War might have made this clear; and the internationally contagious depression that followed upon that policy should certainly have made the impact clear. Further, one might have thought that the international economics of warfare would have certified it. But in any event the problems of international currency stability and the apparent impossibilities of significant rapid economic development in the impoverished states in our present international economy should make this dependence of the national economy upon multinational interaction obvious.

Among other aspects of what we are calling interactively dependent reality are prestige or social standing of the state, political influence of the state, and the military strength of the state. Military strength is often thought of in some abstract absolute quantitative terms (whether they be deliverable megatonnage, number of ICBMs, or any of the other favorite military measures) but this is clearly nothing if it is not a relative quality, as the Vietnam experience confirms in one way, and the debate over nuclear sufficiency offensively and defensively illustrates in another.

Now, what is important about this category of interactively dependent aspects of reality is that, like the other factors, the elements of it are viewed as constraints upon national action, but unlike the others their very existence and strength or direction are directly dependent upon the policies and actions of other states. They are established, in other words, not simply by national actions of all relevant or involved states. Put another way, they are themselves interactive behavior patterns. Reality in these areas consists not of attributes of the state (strength or weakness, capability or incapability), but rather of the patterns of interaction that have been established by the behavior of the involved states in the past and even more significantly by the patterns of interaction that are being either affirmed and hence continued and strengthened by continued consistent actions *or* are being altered by changes in states' actions and hence in interaction.

Thus, in an important sense, the constraints on a nation's behavior lie not in its resources or capabilities or attitudes alone, although these are clearly important elements. Rather, they lie in the established behavior patterns of the interacting states—or, even more accurately, in the beliefs of the participating states about those interactive behavior patterns.

This is why we continue to experience international arms races. Not because states do not realize what analysts have long been pointing out to them: nobody benefits from an arms race; each side is hurt. No country sets out to create an arms race, for each country loses in one: it seeks a relative advantage in military posture but its efforts are met by the other state's countervailing reaction that eliminates or preempts this advantage, and the only real difference is an emptier treasury and perhaps greater insecurity because of higher levels of equaled armament that might be used through accident or miscalculation and in a war would produce greater reciprocal destruction. And it fears a technological breakthrough by the other side and so pours resources into research and development that produce new possibilities that it then feels compelled to exploit, knowing (or believing) that the other party will do the same. Thus the assumptions and desires of each party lead to behavior that creates a new, undesired, and usually unanticipated international reality. These assumptions and desires are components of an image of reality—an image that anticipates hostile threats from others and suggests that these can be most effectively countervailed by increased arming. But the fact that the other state holds the same beliefs—or is led to adopt them when it sees the one state arming against it—creates a process (a "reaction process," as analysts often call it) that "takes control of the situation" and creates a new "reality" or a new image in each state of the inadequacy of its previous efforts. And so each concludes it must begin again. And so it goes.

This "reaction process" is a fundamental component of relations among states in our world, as it is so often among hostile individuals and adversarial social groups. It can be found in the reciprocal escalation in a war such as Vietnam, and it can be found in a long-term general relationship such as that between the United States and the Soviet Union which we generally refer to as the cold war. Particular elements vary, specific reactions and degrees of escalation differ, but the general process persists. And the process, created by the beliefs and desires of the parties involved, alters reality over time. Thus international relations are subject to the same processes of social construction of reality and of reality creation over time to which private interpersonal relations are subject. The manifestations of course vary. Thus the international reality *socially created* over time may be a cold war, or a détente, an arms race, or competitive foreign assistance, or any of the hundreds of happenings that occur because of situations that arise in spite of the policies pursued by states.

We are particularly interested in the process of international reality creation over time. We mean by this not simply, nor even predominantly, those creations resulting from the conscious actions and collaborations of states such as wars, international organizations, or international treaties. There is no question that such efforts alter reality. But in a way, what is most remarkable about them is that they seem so often to fail in their (sometimes internally inconsistent) intended purposes. Wars rarely pay off as hoped; international organizations rarely create the climate and provide the setting for the cooperation they were supposed to encourage; and some treaties are broken while others never attain the significance anticipated because ways are found and used to circumvent them.

Often analysts explain such failings in terms of their being "unrealistic," of their not having taken into account the actual situation (especially the politico-military realities) in the world in which they were created and which they were designed to modify. These are the broad outlines of the explanations of failure and disappointment of the League of Nations and the United Nations, of the Kellogg-Briand Pact outlawing war and the nuclear test moratorium, and of many other venturesome but ill-fated efforts to improve international relations. And we should remember that they are the outlines of the explanations for the failure of less noble efforts, such as the conduct of so many wars.

In addition, and perhaps of even greater importance, such argument about the impossibility or inescapable ineffectuality of so many meliorist measures is a telling blow to efforts to have such changes adopted by states or even considered for proposal by a state. The anticipation of failure, because "the world is not ready for such a measure" or because the revisionist states would deceive and circumvent it, is the most obvious explanation for the otherwise surprising paucity of efforts to alter drastically what almost everyone must agree is a dreadful and treacherous international situation. Some are less troubled than others; but this seems essentially a product of the depth of their conviction of the hostility of reality to major change rather than their endorsement of, or satisfaction with, the prevalence of war and death and privation in our world.

Thus it is crucial that we consider again the validity of the pessimism about the possibility of major constructive change in our present reality as we recollect the failures of so many efforts to change that reality, both constructive and destructive. For it is clear that reality, whatever its state at a given instant, changes constantly. And it is clear that only some of those changes are the consequence of design, of conscious policy and effort by states to alter their reality.

There seem to be many important unintended and unanticipated changes in international reality. These must be the result of developments or processes that we have not yet fully recognized, let alone understood. So we are still a long way from the mastery of them that might renew the prospects for major constructive change in the nature of international relations.

It seems, then, that we must concentrate more upon those nonconscious or undesigned changes or instances of reality creation. If we can understand them better, we may be able to find ways of altering the construction, or perception and comprehension, of reality by states or their policy makers in ways that will not only curtail the incidence of unanticipated undesirable developments, but also discover opportunities for constructive creation of new international reality.

Consciousness of Creation

The prospects are probably substantially better than we might at first suspect. We must remember that international reality is actually constituted over time by the interactions of its participating units, predominantly states (which are, after all, social groups of individuals). Thus this reality is significantly *contingent*—dependent upon the beliefs of individuals, participating as policy makers of states, about its nature. If those beliefs change, reality will change, perhaps in ways that are not at once appreciated by some (or all) participating states. It is this understandable but sometimes forgotten fact that makes possible occasional surprising changes in the international "climate," such as détentes or cold wars.

And obversely, if international reality is to remain relatively stable, these conceptions of reality and the reactions consequent upon them must be maintained. In effect, international reality must be extended or continued, or else it will be re-created. This extension or continuation is often accomplished through a bind of inertia or routine. If states can develop routine responses to acts of other states, they can act without consciously considering or employing their images of reality, and most frequently the actors will have a reinforcing or extending effect on international reality, as in the cases of arms races or a cold war. Thus, in an arms race situation a state has adopted a "routine" or unchanging and unchallenged "program" for responding to the military procurement actions of another by making its military procurement some function of that of the other state. And in the cold war situation a state has a routine or standard interpretation to put upon any action by its adversary—an interpretation that assumes hostility and even malevolence. The same sort of maintenance routine can operate in the opposite direction, in the case of relations among friends who automatically or unquestioningly interpret any action by each other as friendly and hence probably benign.

This sort of routine is important to our understanding of international relations because it is the primary agent by which international reality is given a constancy over time. These routines are important to states because they facilitate efficient policy making and also—precisely because they tend to establish, strengthen, and perpetuate a consistent international reality—because they provide the sense of continuity or stability in the environment that is important for a psychic sense of efficacy.

What must be recognized in addition to this understandable tendency toward routinization and standardized interpretation is the fact of continuing creation. The actions of participating states constitute and reconstitute international reality over time. The sphere of effective action by a state will, of course, be limited by inertias set by material conditions hard to alter. And the range of effective action will be limited to varying degrees by the imagination, the convictions of correctness, and the consciousness of the operation of those reality-creating factors. To each of these we shall return later. But the sphere will also be limited by the practical effects of overarching international processes—processes that so often seem to gain control of policy when one does not wish it. The effects of these processes seem to be the best answer to the question, What explains the frequent failure of conscious efforts to alter international reality, whether by war or international organization? And so it is to an examination of the role of international processes that we must now turn.

chapter five

The Role
of Processes

The best-laid plans of foreign policy makers go oft astray; sometimes through problems of command, control, and communications; sometimes through misperception or misinformation—through difficulties, that is, of internal or national policy making and execution; and sometimes simply because another state proves unexpectedly hostile. But, probably as often, policy failure occurs because the interaction among states which results from the policy's implementation takes a form or has outcomes that are not expected and not controllable.

Problems of Policy

We have a great many ways of naming and characterizing what happens when foreign policy fails. Sometimes we simply say that reality proved intractable; at other times we say that we were, in the intriguing phrase of an investigation of one such mishap (John Bartlow Martin on the Santo Domingo affair), by now quite common in the policy bureaucracy, "overtaken by events" or "OBE." Perhaps the most common term-that-explains is "events take control."

But this term conceals more than it explains. What actually happens is that the early actions of the parties to the affair create a chain of events that *seem to develop a dynamic of their own.* Even this language is too loose to be helpful in our understanding of this most important phenomenon. What happens is that events become patterned—they show a tendency to develop or continue in a certain, regular way. This phenomenon, to which we shall assign the name "process," can happen in one of several ways.

1. In some cases, what we can best understand as routinized *responsive actions are triggered and maintained* by the reciprocal nature of the other party's responsive actions. Such a process can be seen in arms races, for example, in which each party's military procurement, and perhaps budget as well, is consistently made a function or consequence of what is believed to be the other side's procurement and budget. The same phenomenon is found in friendly alliance relations or in the creation and maintenance of a détente among formerly hostile engaged states, where it is simply assumed that one good turn deserves another, or where "like engenders like."

2. In some cases, what occurs is that *actual routines are in fact developed,* so that what could be a series of conscious decisions one like another is actually an almost automated responsive pattern triggered by some recurrent stimulus. All too often, arms races and cold-war relations seem to fall in this category rather than the first, despite their one-would-hope obvious importance. This routinization is a likely consequence of delegation of decision to those less responsive and less imaginative at a time when conventional evidence abounds.

3. But what is basically the same phenomenon of events developing a dynamic of their own can also occur in a rather different way—and one that does bear significant resemblance to "events taking control." In an immediate case, a policy maker, because of his perceptions and understanding and objectives, can perceive (and we can analyze) "the structure

of the situation" as seeming to suggest or even impel a given action.

When we speak of "the structure of the situation" we are referring to the constellation of circumstances or conditions which the policy maker finds himself confronted with and believes are *givens*, features he does not control. Some features are necessarily givens because they are not changeable: the geographic location of states, for example, or the terrain of a battleground. Some of these basically unchangeable features may be compensated for to some extent if they are recognized far enough in advance: technology sometimes overcomes limitations of geography, as in the development of air transportation and high explosives.

But most elements in the structure of the policy-making situation have become givens because *they have become* things the policy maker does not control. Such may occur because he *does not notice* a feature in time, because he *does not appreciate* its degree of *importance* in time, or because he *does not understand the operation* of a process and hence cannot provide for or alter it in advance.

The basic need is, of course, to foresee the phenomenon in time to concentrate and employ the needed resources (attention, talented men, money, military forces, or whatever) to shape or prevent its development so that one preserves his freedom, capability, or escape and thereby de-structures or re-structures the situation.

This formulation suggests that alertness or vigilance might suffice. But such is not usually the case. Two factors must be considered. The first is that attention is inevitably limited. No policy maker can concentrate on everything at once. We have tried to overcome this limitation by "pyramids of concern" in our policy bureaucracies, so that at the lowest level every possible factor is monitored by someone and at higher levels these monitorings are synthesized and reports (intelligence) submitted to those with policy authority. This may help, but thus far it has been essentially unsuccessful, for a rather interesting and very important reason.

We have generally organized our bureaucratic attention in terms of geographic region (with an occasional transcendent qualification such as international organizations or arms control and disarmament). But this structure of both men and attention, and hence of policy, has necessarily assumed that each region is independent of the others—that each subsystem of the international system was "unpenetrated" by other subsystems and their constituent states. This perceptual proclivity is understandable in a superpower which tends to see itself in bilateral relations with each other state or region (thus the United States has, or at least claims to have, a foreign policy toward Chile and a foreign policy toward Latin America). But we are frequently encountering cases in which the components mingle into new overlapping subsystems (thus Chile has a foreign policy toward the Soviet Union and toward Cuba, and vice versa, as well as toward Peru and the United States). This has in the past led to attention structures more assertedly ideological than geographical, such as "the Free World" and "the Communist World," although rather revealingly we have still used geographical terms such as "world" to characterize nongeographical grouping. Such an approach has been inadequate, and obviously so, and efforts have more recently been designed to "correct" this orientation by emphasizing bilateral analysis (that is, America's relations with each of 130-odd states), but this has again made it more difficult to foresee and appreciate the importance of relations between, for example, the Soviet Union and the People's Republic of China for each country's relations with Chile which in turn are so important for Chile's relations with the United States.

The point is not that one cannot see this in the abstract,

but rather that our policy process is poorly structured to enable our policy to reflect this importance by at once viewing our relations with each country as interrelated with our relations with the others and relations among them, and so making our policy toward each a function of all these other relations— ours and theirs. We simply do not know how to do this—at least not yet. And because we do not, our attention is limited or focused in ways that make a given policy situation descend upon or arrive at us as *structured*—characterized by many important features that we cannot in fact shape or influence because we realize their interrelated importance too late.

This brings us to—and is even an example of—the second crucial factor in understanding how situations become so structured. Many processes are presently *tendencies*, or developments with momentum or an inclination or dynamic, and hence must be consciously controlled or deflected if they are not to dominate by structuring the decision situation for the decision maker. (We shall examine the more interesting of such processes below.)

Furthermore, it can be the case that not only is the situation structured so that it apparently denies the policy maker freedom of choice, but also the actual structure is such that for practical purposes it virtually guarantees the failure of the action the policy maker feels compelled to take. Given certain objectives and certain types of situations, a policy maker can find himself "locked in" so that he believes he must act in a certain way *but* the only available or recognized actions are self-defeating—they render the objective unattainable.

The Domination of Policy by Process

Many of the effects of international interaction can be best understood as process consequences. That is to say, whatever policy makers and analysts believe about the merits of American policy on Vietnam or ABM or military aid to Greece, they can probably all agree that the price in death and hunger and illness paid by peasants throughout the less developed countries with major political conflict is much too high, that the arms race between the United States and the Soviet Union has long been too accelerated and at levels that are too high, and that the militarization of foreign aid programs distorts foreign economics and often exacerbates regional tensions.

This agreement, then, is on the misfortune that results from processes of interaction that characterize much of international relations—processes such as the reaction process underlying arms races; the tendency of insurgency/counter-insurgency wars to develop into destruction of life and welfare of rural peoples unenthusiastic about the issues underlying the conflict; and the disruptions to local economies and regional balances that military aid engenders.

These are examples of processes engendered in international relations not at all purposely and indeed probably in most cases contrary to the wishes of the interacting states. Furthermore, and more importantly, they are *consequences even of successful policies* and actions; counterinsurgency afflicts large numbers of peasants even if it is successful; ABM programs intensify arms races even if they are miraculously confined to defensive postures and prove successful in strengthening the defense of the parties; and military aid distorts local economies and creates regional arms races even if —indeed, perhaps especially if—it is successful in strengthening the military position of the state aided. It is important to understand the processes at work in this confounding of objectives.

Generally speaking, American foreign policy, like that of other states, is directed primarily at particular objectives or stakes. These objectives or stakes tend to take the form of state and territorial "integrity"—our own and others'. Thus ABM assertedly protects our retaliatory capability that itself deters the Soviet Union from threatening our territory. And thus our effort in Vietnam assertedly protects the territory of South Vietnam against incursions from North Vietnam as well as the security of "our Southerners" against threats from "theirs." And thus military aid to Greece strengthens that state as a NATO ally against threats from Communist states.

The fact that our foreign policy and the actions taken in consonance with or to implement it concentrate upon objectives or stakes conceived usually in territorial terms is hardly surprising. But its impact is crucial. For our concentration upon stakes is necessarily at the expense of attention to processes.

The actions we take to secure or obtain and maintain particular stakes in the world inevitably create and/or strengthen particular processes of international relations, for these processes are compounds of actions by one state and responses or actions by another state (or states). If these processes were simply *and only* such compounds, they would not be any less real than they are, but they might be more controllable. Unfortunately they are not only simple compounds of actions. Rather, they often develop what can best be understood as their own momentum—a dynamic that exacerbates their rate of development.

We know this phenomenon quite well in the common cases of what are usually termed "reaction processes" such as the arms race and hostility escalations in interpersonal relations, and a similar phenomenon is manifest in the multiplier effects in economic change. Such common phenomena share this dynamic feature, not because they become "things in themselves" charging off to reshape the world. Rather, as we well know, they exist because the components (international adversaries, parties to the economic marketplace, blacks and whites, or whoever) are closely related to each other in an interacting system, and the actions of each are in part at least responsive to the actions of others. And when those reactions are largely protective, assuming (to protect against it) the worst possible case or at least a bad one, the process is hastened considerably.

In other words, these processes have a dynamic "reality creating" effect, especially when perceptions by those involved are influenced by fear or love or other "filters." The processes also tend to give off, as a kind of sediment, an "environment," or beliefs about the nature of reality at the time, that we often refer to in the case of international relations as "the climate" or "an atmosphere" or "a spirit." And our beliefs about the international climate or atmosphere are then fed back into our policy making and action in the form of claims about the nature of international reality, the will of adversaries and allies, which help us determine "the limits of the possible" as policy makers and advisers so often like to put it.

Because we know this effect can be important, we try to remain conscious of our assumptions. But as policy is made, what attention the processes created receive seems often to be misdirected.

For example, because we want to improve the tenor or nature of international relations, we decide that we must concentrate upon the process of "aggression," and particularly what we perceive to be the escalatory process by which the more a hungry state is allowed to obtain, the more it will want and the more risks it will believe it safe to take. Such an analysis can lead to a conclusion that aggression must be stopped whenever and wherever it occurs and by whatever means necessary, including major force. In consequence, this process interest, then, shifts almost imperceptibly from a concern with the process of escalating desires to the immediate stake of defending a particular piece of territory. This transition underlies the American response in Korea, which was supported in part by the claim that it would make fighting elsewhere in Asia unnecessary by raising the price of aggression and thereby educating potential aggressors as well as the actual aggressor in the case at hand. Nonetheless, we subsequently had Vietnam, which was designed to do the same thing, believed necessary because of the operation of the "domino theory." Such a process seems likely to be continually sustained, in part because the effort to execute a policy designed to eliminate the process inescapably extends and even strengthens that very process.

What is occurring here merits further examination. Explaining the tendency of process goals concerning the nature or "tenor" of the international environment or of international relations in general to become converted into territorial goals requires some attention to mentality and some to experience. There seems to be a tendency for people to prefer territorial goals to process goals, and to convert process goals into territorial goals because territorial goals are easier to understand and pursue. They require less sophisticated and mentalistic conception, and they tend to involve less human complication. Furthermore, the great emphasis on territorial stakes in the cold war era, following the very territorial Second World War and interspersed with the Korean war, has tended to socialize all of us into a highly territorial view of international politics. The rhetoric about "the struggle for the hearts and minds of men" has been uttered in support of policies directed toward maintaining or capturing the territory of men.

This effect is perhaps most poignantly seen in our apparent agonizing inability to see the nonterritorial aspects of the war in Vietnam. It is not simply that we trained the South Vietnamese army to fight a conventional territorial war and ourselves showed singular difficulty adjusting to the political and nonterritorial aspects of waging the struggle. In addition, and perhaps even more fundamentally, we insisted on seeing the war as *essentially* an invasion rather than an unconventional civil war with external participation. The contribution of this monumental misunderstanding and the tragedy of the policy we based upon it have been well portrayed elsewhere. The consequences of our "socialization" by the territorial emphases of previous wars and our view of the cold war—especially when built upon the education we received from our academic and publicist "Realists"—have not yet been fully realized. They tend to convert what might otherwise look like sheer belligerent malevolence into a historic Greek tragedy.

No such account, of course, does justice to the complexity and unclarity of motives and forces underlying particular policies and actions. But it can remind us of the tendency to shift attention from process to stakes. We know that processes shape international relations, even as actions directed toward particular stakes cumulate into processes. And we know that processes account for and construct the major misfortunes in the contemporary international political world—the pervasive violence and "illfare" that even our policy makers deplore.

Furthermore, we can see that the general criticisms now directed at American foreign policy do not address this issue. Generally, they argue that we should decrease the extent or dispersion and number of stakes we seek. But if they promise any process effect, it may well be what the harshest adversaries of these critics fear: a process effect of withdrawal encouraging greater instability, greater venturesomeness in some hostile quarters, and greater ultimate vulnerability in our position.

The Nature of Processes in Policy and Politics

We are not likely to be able to get beyond this sort of revealing but quite specific policy analysis unless we pay more attention to the nature of such processes and examine briefly but specifically major processes that seem to shape foreign policy and international relations.

We must first demystify the concept of "process." Among the definitions of "process" in the Oxford English Dictionary are the following:

> Something that goes on or is carried on; a continuous action, or series of actions or events; a course or method of action, proceeding, procedure.

> A continuous and regular action or succession of actions, taking place or carried on in a definite manner, and leading to the accomplishment of some result; a continuous operation or series of operations. (The chief current sense.) A natural or involuntary operation; a series of changes or movements taking place.

This set of definitions reveals in a helpful but too general way the features of processes as we shall use the term. Any process must be a *series* of actions or events (or, at one level, of thoughts), with a pattern or regularity of some sort (without which we would never even be inclined to class the events as a series). The nature of this pattern or regularity may vary, however, from case to case. The regular series must also have an effective *automaticity* or tendency to exist as a patterned series—perhaps (in the case of a pernicious process) because its nature or operation is unrecognized or unperceived, or perhaps because it is continuous unless consciously altered or stopped—whatever the mechanism or structure of things responsible for this automaticity. The process *may* also *have a dynamism*—a tendency to change in rate or scale—such as that characteristic of escalatory processes underlying arms races or friendship. Thus a process is taken to be a series of actions or events, with a pattern or regularity and an effective automaticity, sometimes dynamic.

But while this crude definition helps us to decide which phenomena merit inclusion, it also tends to reify the concept in a way that could prove seriously misleading. Thus we must now demystify "process" by recollecting that it is a descriptive ascription to something that tends to happen because of the orientations of people. That is, processes do not really take control; rather, people relinquish control and thereby create processes. They do this for quite understandable reasons of routine, busyness, learned (educated) proclivity, or choice of policy for other reasons that sets in motion a chain of events or creates the new compelling series of "structured situations" in which freedom of action seems not to exist.

Another way of viewing this is to see that processes are rooted in and develop out of actors' continuing *dispositions in structured situations*. Either the disposition or the structure of the situation may seem most important in explaining a specific instance of the phenomenon. When behavior varies or would vary from one to another actor in the given situation, we direct our attention to disposition. When there is no reason to expect or suspect such interactor variation, we are likely to be more concerned with the structure of the situation —at least if we are attempting to explain a particular instance, although perhaps not if we are desirous of developing a way of changing things (of changing, in other words, the processes that are responsible for the extension of the actor dispositions over time).

Such abstract definition, conceptualization, and analysis may not advance our understanding of the phenomena of foreign policy and international relations at this point, but it will become quite helpful when we attempt to find ways to control processes. The next step toward that goal is to examine in greater array the processes with which we may be concerning ourselves in our study of foreign policy and international politics.

Types of Processes in Policy and Politics

The processes that may interest us can be organized and examined in various ways, but for our purposes the most useful classification will be in terms of the actors involved.

Two categories of processes arise in a single individual. The *cognitive* processes are those affecting the operation of the thought capacities of the mind, including the affective and the unconscious as well as the perceptual and the data processing activities of the mind. The *mental* processes are those affecting the conscious thought of the mind. These two categories are in practice somewhat arbitrary in their distinctiveness and even more so in their terminology. We shall have occasion to examine certain elements of them when we consider the images of individuals. That subject will be introduced in the next chapter, and further specification and examination of these processes will be deferred until then.

The next major group of processes is constituted by those that occur in the policy making and execution of a single actor (generally, in our case, a state). There are a great many such processes, six of which seem of particular promise for our inquiry into the determinants of international reality over time.

The first is *distortion of communication*. We know from the study of communication that as information is passed from person to person (or even, often, from machine to machine), it is likely to be eroded or distorted by such factors as "noise," translation or paraphrase, and memory lapse. Such phenomena occur regularly in policy making, as accounts consistently indicate. Indeed, the phenomena are so frequent and so inescapable that we seem justified in viewing such distortion of communication as a significant process. But we must also remember that such distortion will vary considerably from one culture to another.

A second process that can afflict or more accurately influence decision making is *decision process domination*. The necessity to formulate a problem for decision, the preparation of an agenda, the operant rules for resolution of conflict (such as the use of majority vote, operation by parliamentary procedures, etc.) and the operation of other "rules of the game" that will vary from unit to unit and perhaps even case to case—such factors can be grouped for our purpose into a tendency for the decision process itself to influence or even dominate the substantive policy outcome. This process will vary in strength or importance with the collegiality of the body and the way it operates, but in some cases it can be very important in understanding policy outcomes—especially if it is combined with the fourth process, bureaucratic politicking.

The third process is objective or *goal rigidification*. We have considered above the tendency for American policy to convert "environmental" or process goals into territorial stakes. This is an example of the more general phenomenon whereby factors such as a felt need for constancy (for "having a policy" for everything), elements in shared human experience or socialization or education, etc., may operate to rigidify a goal. Another factor in such rigidification, rather different and perhaps more important, but more closely related to particular policies, strategies, and tactics, is the belief in the importance of making and then maintaining commitments—a commitment being a move by which a party puts itself in a position where it must do something it would on-the-immediate-merits prefer not to do. And there are various others, one of the more intriguing general ones being the tendency of debate and understanding and hence policy toward a lowest-common-denominator conventional wisdom.

The fourth process is the tendency toward *bureaucratic*

politicking in policy making. Bureaucratic politicking incorporates competition for personal objectives and rewards (such as one's place in the history books or a more powerful position in the organization) and for objectives and rewards favorable to one's subsystem (contests of interorganizational or intersystem rivalry, for example—contests that often play upon participants' senses of loyalty, however divided or unitary). The crucial feature of such bureaucratic politicking is that it takes place at the immediate expense of the major unit or system's external objectives (as a quarrel between the Executive Office of the president and the State Department can afflict and has affected American foreign policy)—even though it is sometimes asserted to be in the longer-run interests of the system (as with interservice rivalry in the military). Such politicking can be particularly important, for example, in determining who decides, especially in a crisis when there is a tendency to shrink the number of participants in decision. Other examples are legion.

The fifth process is *routinization of action*. We have already examined the nature and suggested the incidence of routinization. It is clearly essential for policy making (rather as habits are essential to the individual if he is to cope effectively with the multitudinous demands of everyday life), but it has the potentiality for significantly affecting policy adversely and long remaining undiscovered precisely because of its routine nature.

The sixth process is the tendency of *support changes* that are often termed the "bandwagon effect" (in which previous opponents move to support something because they see it will win and want to be on the winning side, thereby increasing its support inordinately, independent of their beliefs about its actual merits, and incidentally invalidating forecasts at the same time) and the "underdog effect" (the obverse, in which supporters desert something out of sympathy for the apparent loser, thereby altering the constellation of support if not necessarily the decision itself). Such processes, when they operate, can affect either decision itself or external support for it, and either effect can be important for our analysis of foreign policy making and execution.

The other major group of processes is that of interaction processes. The policy processes we have just briefly catalogued have their interaction counterparts. Thus there can be (and usually seems to be) a *misunderstanding* process in relations among major systems deriving from the same communications problems that cause distortion in policy making. There may also be *procedural* processes operant in diplomatic interaction. *Rigidification* of objective tends to occur whenever states interact, and is intensified by the fact of public attentiveness and beliefs about the importance of facts and credibility of commitment. The phenomenon we analyze as bureaucratic politicking at the state level is actually in its essentials what we generally conceive to be the essence of state interaction in which we find *national interest dominance* over common interest among states. *Routinization*, as we have seen, is an essential component of the "tenor" of relations over time that we refer to as cold war, détente, or whatever. *Support processes* resembling the bandwagon and underdog effects are of the essence in alliance politics, and can affect other interstate politics where more than two states are involved.

But the interaction processes we are most familiar with are, of course, the reaction processes that form the basis of arms races, cold warring, wartime escalation, détente development, and almost any less striking alteration of the nature of relations. We have previously examined these processes briefly, and there seems to be no misunderstanding of them, so that we can postpone further attention to them until we are ready to develop ways of reconstructing international relations. For the moment we need only recollect that the processes may be constant (linear) or magnifying (exponential) in their development, and that they may tend toward integration or at least cooperation (the latter if there is no dynamic or routinization that drives the cooperation toward integration), or they may tend toward disintegration or at least conflict. We shall return to these crucial reaction processes.

An Approach to the Study of Processes

Most criticism of the state of international relations takes the form of criticism of the international environment—its violence content, the "illfare" resulting from the nature of relations among states, etc.—as these features relate to the needs and desires of the country and its people. But as we have seen, environmental developments are in large measure determined by the operation of international processes.

Such processes as we have been examining actually constitute and create international reality over time. Partly this is a result of the ways in which they shape interaction over time; partly it results from the dynamic or momentum, so characteristic of processes, that provides the "engine" by which "events take control"; and partly it results from the fact that processes leave in their wake a kind of "sediment," beliefs about the international climate or atmosphere at the time, which in turn creates the environment within which the policy maker operates.

Because of this, we obviously need a greater knowledge of the nature and operation of such processes and their effects if we are to understand better what transpires in international relations. Furthermore, there must be a greater consciousness of these processes and their effect on the part of policy makers and advocates, if they are to increase their creative development or even merely to improve execution of present policies.

This knowledge must include recognition that the processes are sometimes uncontrollable and often uncontrolled. In a sense, there is always one or more process at work creating reality over time. A key question is how "coherent" it is (in the sense that a laser beam is "coherent light"). There are many examples of consciously designed coherent processes. Planning, especially economic planning by a state, is now an accepted form of exerting control over and even actually generating process effects toward a particular goal such as increasing gross national product, controlling expansion of an economic sector, or developing a particular functional capability in a society. The drive for "strategic superiority" militarily by the United States in the years of Soviet-American rivalry is an example of a combination of such planning with a not-wholly-controlled dynamic process.

Some such processes can be developed, and others that exist already in a particular international situation can be made more coherent (rather in the way that a nuclear reaction can be controlled). Exactly which processes operate and whether they are benign (beneficent) or malignant (malevolent) will depend upon the assumptions about the nature of reality made by the parties involved, including especially the understanding of the structural features of the situation (both bureaucratic and environmental).

But this will also depend upon the parties' consciousness or realization that the processes operate and their consequent policy of controlling them. States cannot effectively control processes without recognizing their imminence or operation. The absence of such recognition can be an important element in explaining the pervasiveness and virulence of local arms races that do nobody any good. Such recognition can help to explain what success has been had in controlling some arms races by agreement explicit or tacit.

Such consciousness will not necessarily succeed, however, for the coherence of processes, whether beneficent or malevolent, and their controllability, will be complicated immensely by certain features of our complex international relations. Among these critical features are the existence of different countries, of different interests in each country (united in seeking "profit" of some sort, but at odds because such profit often must be obtained at one another's expense), and of different people in charge in each country—a factor somewhat lessened by the Americanization of the rest of the world (a development in turn consequent upon the homogenizing effect of our culture).

These factors contribute, along with knowledge and whatever consciousness exists, to determining the limits of control or influence a country can exercise over the processes we are examining.

But the way in which such control or influence arises, given consciousness, is through the images or conceptions of reality possessed by decision makers and advisers. If there is a way of influencing the impact of the processes, it is through these reality images, which are after all the roots of the dispositions that result in action. Images or conceptions—of such elements as personal responsibility and opportunity, bureaucratic politics and the rules of the game, as well as the nature of the international atmosphere or environment and the nature and interests of adversaries—influence objectives and shape actions that actually compose the interactions out of which these processes "arise."

Thus, in a sense, processes and reality images are linked in a feedback loop in which each is affected by changes in the other. As a scholar or a policy advocate, one may cut into this loop at any point. Most such efforts cut into subsidiary elements such as state objectives or ongoing international political phenomena such as war or crisis. This results in a necessarily superficial and conditional understanding—one that may suffice if one's primary interest is studying the pattern of a particular phenomenon or recommending ways to greater efficiency.

But such approaches have not generally aided us in discovering opportunities for systemic change. The understanding of international processes is an important prerequisite for such innovation. But even this is insufficient for several reasons. First, if our chief objective is understanding what transpires we are inevitably limited if not crippled by the mechanical imagery and focus of process analysis. What we require for satisfactory understanding is a human or "experiential" analysis that enables us to comprehend the meaning of decisions for those making them. Only then can we succeed in resolving our own puzzles about why they behaved as they did, and thereupon begin to assess their own conceptions of their decision situations in terms of what we believe those situations to be—perhaps because of our greater knowledge and consciousness of the operations of processes.

This then brings us to the second reason for the need to examine more than processes. Process analysis abstracts from decision as such, and this makes its usefulness in discovering possibilities for control of those processes less than obvious. Again, only a better understanding of the decisional situation might advance us in this search.

Thus we are led toward the examination of reality images because they promise to be both a better road to understanding the human action that cumulates into internal and international political processes and a potential entrance into the ultimate mastery of those processes as far as that may prove possible. What, then, do we know and can we learn about such reality images?

chapter six

The Importance of Images

Dispositions, Actions, and Processes

Each of us is a bundle of dispositions. A disposition, in this sense, is a tendency and a readiness to perceive, interpret, expect, or act in some particular way. Such mental sets are the necessary products of our physiology and our experience, and they are important because they influence what we perceive and the significance we attribute to it, as well as how we act, over and above the "merits of the situation." The presence of different dispositions in different individuals in the same circumstances accounts for their viewing and acting differently, even as the presence of changed dispositions in the same individual in similar circumstances at different times can account for his different action.

Such dispositions thus make possible and give direction to the actions of an individual. In chapter 5 we defined a process as a series of actions or events with a pattern or regularity and an effective automaticity. And we saw that processes can be seen as rooted in and developing out of continuing actor dispositions in structured situations. Such processes are constituted by actions, but the actions are informed by dispositions.

Thus, when we seek to explain a decision, an action, or an event in terms of its determinants, we may be inclined to search for the dispositions of the actor(s) involved. Four categories of dispositions may be of special interest to us.

1. *Perception dispositions* are those dispositions that influence what one actually sees, hears, feels, or otherwise perceives. They may be inherent in the organism as the tendency toward completion of the visual field is asserted to be by Gestalt psychologists. Or they may be learned or conditioned.

2. But many of the dispositions often considered perceptual by analysts of foreign policy making are more helpfully understood as *comprehension dispositions*. These are the inclinations and tendencies, often masquerading as "rules of thumb" or "hypotheses," which the individual uses to understand the *significance* or *meaning* of what he perceives. Without such interpretation, an individual would be unable to cope with, let alone remember and make use of, the vast flood of perceptions he receives or achieves. This comprehension is composed of and by elements of the individual's socialization, education, and other life experience. Socialization is especially important as a source of interpretation concerning people, as education is important concerning social roles and ideas. One's life experience permits and specifies the socialization and education in ways that are so complex and various that we do not yet understand them well. All we can be certain about is that this set of comprehension dispositions is crucial to the actor's ability to function in an otherwise unbearably chaotic world, and it plays a major role in accounting for interpersonal and intergroup differences in what analysts often rather casually refer to as "perception."

3. The third important element is *expectation dispositions*. We know intuitively that some people are optimists and others pessimists. We know that some people continually expect some event to occur or some particular fortune to befall them. These and other such expectations are elements in one's attitude toward the future. This attitude shapes particular as

well as general expectations. As we shall see, one's image of the future and the expectation disposition underlying it—an image of the possible, the likely, the desirable and the undesirable, the avoidable and the unavoidable—can be crucial and essential determinants of, or at least influences upon, what does eventually take place. Thus we shall frequently return our attention to the expectation disposition.

4. The final major category with which we are especially concerned is *action dispositions*. This set includes one's general sense of efficacy and one's tendency to act or not to act in particular types of situations. The disposition derives from one's personality as well as one's rules about effective action (what works, if anything does, in various given types of situations, often with reference to other actors).

We may well find ourselves inclined to explain particular decisions and actors in terms of such dispositions. Most explanation by disposition has generally taken some form of reference to human nature—that is, to what all people have in common—rather than to idiosyncratic dispositions. Most people recognize that expectation and action tendencies obviously differ among individuals, but each tends to assume that *he* understands *accurately* rather than *determinedly*, just as he will assume he perceives accurately rather than as a consequence of some particular set, however it is determined. Thus one tends to believe that all people can (and should) agree upon comprehension—such as the significance of an act, or the structure of a situation.

It is exactly these common assumptions that make explanation by disposition appealing, for showing that expectations, comprehensions, or perceptions differed can help to remove our puzzlement at particular actions. When we engage in such explanation by disposition, we attempt to show how an actor's dispositions were triggered or invoked in a particular set of experienced circumstances and the actor thereupon applied his own theories of how to act effectively in circumstances such as those he believed himself in and so made a particular decision or took a particular action.

Such explanation by disposition can obviously be helpful in coping with puzzlement about particular instances of decision and action. But explanation by disposition suffers from a crucial difficulty. It is behavioral rather than experiential—that is, it must rely on the behavior of an individual for its information about his action. We have no direct way to uncover dispositions beyond either asking a person how he is disposed (a remarkably unreliable approach, as any who have tried it can attest, not necessarily because subjects are deceitful but rather because they are so often highly unreflective or unself-conscious) or by making inferences from his behavior. But it is that very behavior, or at least a particular instance of it, that we are attempting to explain.

Thus there is a strong incentive to seek an *experiential* rather than a behavioral approach. An experiential approach would concentrate upon the experience of the individual as he decides and acts—primarily the structure of the situation as he sees it and the meaning of his action to him. We discover this structure and meaning in essentially the same ways as we do his dispositions—by asking him and making inferences from his behavior. But we have two crucial advantages when doing such experiential explanation rather than behavioral explanation.

First, we are seeking information about what is in his conscious mind (structure and meaning) rather than something that is not likely to be in his conscious mind (his perceptual, comprehension, expectation, and action dispositions), so we are more likely to receive the information we seek from him.

Second, because we have conscious minds with experience at deciding in various situations, we can better comprehend or interpret his behavior in terms of the information it offers about his conscious decision, and we can check what he says and what his behavior implies about his experience in deciding against what we as fellow human beings know about the experience of deciding and acting.

The fact, then, that we have a considerable advantage as fellow human beings in attempting to understand the experience of an individual deciding, even if we have never been in the same decision situation, does not suggest that our task will be easy, but only that it is likely to be easier than that of explaining and understanding that act while concentrating upon or limiting ourselves to behavioral evidence.

The quest for dispositional explanations is such an essentially behavioral quest. But because we well know that such dispositions are crucial to, and crucially close to, decisions we will want to explain, we are encouraged to find another entrance into the decision process that is less limiting. This is one of the considerations that leads us to focus upon the *images of reality* held by the decision maker.

The Importance of Reality Images

A "reality image" is the picture or image of the nature of reality that one holds in his mind. The major elements of a reality image that will be of special concern to us are three:

1. The *image of the world* that surrounds the individual and hence provides the environment for his action, including the actions of others. This image of the world will generally include some picture or sense of trends or directions of major change in the world at a time when change is endemic to social life and the social world. Thus the image of the world will consist largely of description coupled with whatever explanatory theory the individual has been able to develop and receive. It is this image of the world that enables one facing a

decision to develop or construct his "definition of the situation."

2. The image of the world as it must be—a reality beyond actuality—provides the individual with some basis for assessing what he finds surrounding him and for grounding his own actions in a set of *values* for application. These values will be derived from what amounts to value theory. Traditionally, those studying decision have treated values either as an absolute somewhere outside of the individual's image of reality, or else as nothing more than a positive element like any other in his reality. Actually, values seem best viewed differently, as the element of a man's reality image that asserts itself as a basis for valuation and action and even for understanding because it is grounded in the Natural Order of Things, the Way the World Works, the Will of God, Human Nature, or whatever. Every man has some such value principle or theory, whether he realizes it or not. It is a part of his reality image, and it must be discovered and exploited or changed if he is to be understood or influenced.

3. The final major element in any reality image is the image of *effective action principles* and opportunities that constitutes the "engineering theory" or "operating theory" that he can employ in attempting to achieve what he values in the world that he perceives and in which he therefore believes he must operate.

These three elements—image of the world, image of value, and image of effective action—combine to constitute the reality image of any man. Because each man is different genetically and biographically from all other men, there will be differences in reality images from one man to another. These differences may range from practically insignificant (in men with similar genes and socialization, education, and experience) to very extensive.

All human interaction (as well as much interaction between a man and his material environment) concerns reality images, first because one's action derives from one's reality image and second because one's action asserts one's reality image to others and implicitly recommends it for others' consideration. And because each individual is different, virtually all interaction is grounded in and concerns *differing* reality images.

This difference over the nature of reality provides the basis for politics in our society. For politics can best be seen and understood as *dispute over claims to authority concerning the nature of reality*. Clearly no individual can discover everything for himself and few can even develop their own method of inquiry by means of which to discover reality and in the results of which they can have adequate confidence. For most of us most of the time there is a persistent but generally latent question of authority: On whom should one rely for his method of determining what reality is, and especially on whom should one rely for substantive assertions about the nature of reality? There is also often the further question concerning public policy: On whom should one rely for action and policy concerning that reality?

The power of a view of reality resides ultimately in a claim about the Natural Order of Things, Human Nature, God's Will, or whatever absolute is unassailable. But in a society like ours (whether we be concerned with America for Americans or with "the society of states" for America) in which there no longer is such an authority, the claims about reality must be supported intellectually.

Popular skepticism about intellectual claims to authority in our country is compounded by the general belief that intellectuals have been irrelevant and incompetent in solving "real world" problems of the economy, of peace and war, etc. And thus is created the basis for and need for politics. For the function politics performs is to provide the *possibility of authority* that can obviate or obliterate this pervasive societal weakness.

Politics, then, as we view it, is the dispute over claims to authority concerning reality images—images of the world, of values, and of operating principles for achieving what one's values recommend. Because reality images differ with differing genetics, biographies, and current perspectives, and because there is no universally accepted authority to resolve these differences, we have politics—interpersonally, locally, nationally, and above all internationally.

This then is a critical reason for our concentration upon reality images: they form the basis for the authority controversies that constitute what we know as politics.

There are other reasons as well for our focus on reality images. We have already seen (in our discussion of dispositions as a possible focus) that images have an advantage for us in that they are elements of the conscious mind that are therefore potentially accessible to their holders and both comprehensible and often more accessible to observers, since all humans have images and to varying extents know that they do.

But of much greater interest to our basic effort in this study, to understand why world politics develop as they do and what might be done to improve them significantly, are three other reasons for studying reality images: (1) images of international reality tend to create and alter international reality over time; (2) images of reality are ultimately or basically socially generated and hence potentially socially changeable; and (3) such change in images will depend upon a greater consciousness of the role of images in creating reality and the role of individuals in creating images. Both of these recommend attention to *conscious* phenomena such as reality images, rather than often *unconscious* phenomena such as dispositions, or *nonconscious* phenomena such as social processes. We must now examine each of these arguments for the importance of studying reality images.

The Impact of Reality Images on International Reality

Our examination of the continuous creation of international reality has already suggested that the reality images of policy makers can be instrumental in shaping international relations because they influence conduct in ways that can be self-confirming or self-denying. The important point should be quite clear: reality images, whatever their material bases, whatever their momentary justification, can be critical determinants of what happens in international relations, even to the extent of altering the very international reality about which they are a statement of belief. This is a supremely important reason for studying reality images with great care and greater imagination.

The Social Construction of International Reality Images

Another closely linked reason for studying reality images is that these images are socially generated and so are potentially quite alterable.

If reality images were basically only reflections of ongoing material and relational reality, they would change or could be changed only as that reality changed. Thus material factors such as technological change and economic development, and relational factors such as reaction processes, would be the major if not the only possible agents that could change reality images, as they were reflected in the more superficial "educational" process by which information about these material and rational changes in reality would be brought to the attention of people. In this instance there would almost certainly be a "behavior lag" as policy makers gradually absorbed knowledge of technological, economic, and other changes and painfully adjusted their reality images and consequently their routines for developing and assessing policy.

In fact, this account is probably an approximately accurate description of what generally influences the reality images of policy makers and their advisers, critics, and students. Most of us today seem to cling to a naive view of reality as not only relatively unchanging but even further not significantly subject to change by the images of it held by actors. And thus the efforts of most analysts such as policy makers are to attune their images of reality to "what is really out there." We have seen that this view tends to be somewhat self-fulfilling in the sense that it surrenders most of the possibility of our controlling reality by controlling our images of reality.

Most importantly, it ignores and even attempts to deny the fact that both our images of reality and reality itself are in crucial ways socially generated. We have seen above various ways in which not only relational reality but even material reality is socially generated. The primary mechanism for this creation of reality is our own "imaging" of reality.

The closest we ever come to "knowing what reality is" is achieving interpersonal agreement on "what reality is." The essence of this process is to be found in our socialization system, which includes everything from the experiences we foist upon our infants through formal schooling to adult experiences of the media and exposures to authority figures.

We generate proximate agreement about international relations and our state's place in the world through development of national consciousness in a growing child. We couple placing him geographically with indoctrinating him with a simplistic patriotism that at best generally takes the form of unquestioned nationalism, and often degenerates into militant and aggressive chauvinism. The result of such socialization is not only a parcel of attitudes about public questions, but also

—and ultimately more importantly—a set of beliefs about international reality that has as its source those attitudes, but has implications that transcend the attitudes and usually survive their discrediting.

At this stage, our concern is not to criticize our socialization, but rather to see how it contributes to creation of a social consensus on the nature of international reality. This consensus then constitutes international reality in the sense most meaningful to an actor or his critic, for it enables one to make policy or recommendations in accordance with shared beliefs about the environment in which one acts. When policy fails, it may be criticized for being based on false ("unrealistic") beliefs about international reality. But more often it is criticized for poor formulation or implementation. And thus the virtual consensus on the nature of international reality can remain unchallenged even when events, the harshest elements of reality, might in effect be attempting to criticize that prevailing reality image by thwarting the policy based on it.

It is important to see that the development of a consensus on the nature of reality takes place, informally and perhaps usually nonconsciously, among whatever individuals or groups are parties to interaction in the context of that reality. Thus, while a state's foreign policy is generated by individuals within the state, it is influenced by the actions of other states. And this interaction, not merely among states but among policies, provides the basis for yet another possible consensus on international reality: that among states.

We have suggested that politics can be best understood as dispute over authority claims concerning reality images. Thus it is that typically there will be less dispute within a state about its foreign policy than there will be between states. Bipartisanship, assertions of popular ignorance and official expertise, etc., all contribute to agreement within a state upon foreign policy by strengthening the claims to authority of the

professional policy makers. They grow out of the pervasiveness of socialization within the state coupled with the high degree of acceptance of the authority of officials by the public.

But matters are generally quite different internationally, for most states lack shared pervasive socialization and there is precious little mutually recognized authority. International politics are usually more virulent and less bounded than national politics, for while the claims to authority by the various states are strong, the recognition of that authority in defining the essential world reality is scarce. What is at issue, again, is the establishment of a consensus on international reality. The contest is pursued by parties with differing worldviews. Their competition often turns into conflict. The explanation for this is quite complex, but it derives in part from the lack of conscious attention to one's own and others' reality images. We shall see that there are hidden here great opportunities for the improvement of international relations.

The Changeability of Reality Images

The final major reason for concentrating attention on reality images is their changeability. Because reality images are elements of the conscious mind (even if one is not always conscious of his image of reality), they can be examined and appealed to intellectually and verbally. Dispositions, because they are not so clearly conscious, are generally subject only to mechanical training or manipulation. Thus the movement from dispositions toward images as the focus of our study is a movement from training, conditioning, and routine toward consciousness.

We, like many others, have rendered a negative assessment of the consequences for international relations of policies and actions undertaken on the basis of present reality images and without a careful and imaginative consciousness of the impact of these reality images upon reality. It is the

clear implication of this negative assessment, that a greater consciousness of this is a real hope, and perhaps the only great hope, for "civilizing" not only our foreign policy but international relations as well. If we are to improve our way of relating to our world, we must become more conscious first of what our reality images are, then of how to manage or control our own images constructively, and finally of how to influence the images and hence the behavior of other states to bring about cooperation in the reconstruction of international politics.

The Relevant Study of Reality Images

International relations are obviously social in the sense that they will involve at least two parties interacting. They are also much more fundamentally social in the sense that they consist of interactions not between two monolithic actors, the states, but actually between two groups of representatives of those states, be they diplomats, soldiers, or citizens. Furthermore, international relations are social because they result from foreign policy making and such policy making is inescapably a collective venture. Whatever the policy process, whether strictly collegial or serially and hierarchically collective, it must involve individuals with differing perceptions and comprehensions (because of differing perspectives and biographies as well as differing competences) *and* with differing responsibilities (in all but the strictest egalitarian collegial case) and with differing responsivenesses. These conditions make both international relations among several states and foreign policy making within a state subject to the same general processes of the social construction of reality and of reality creation over time.

Because this is true, if we wish to understand the nature of international reality we must realize three things: (1) it is a product of the actions of states; (2) it consists in mutable patterns of interactive behavior; (3) it is created and can be changed only if we can devise ways in which nations may alter their behavior such that it will contribute to alteration of patterned reality not merely by altering their component of the interaction but also by enticing others to modify their components of the interaction in a way compatible with this alteration. That way, both alterations taken together will contribute to establishment of a new, mutually preferred pattern of interaction, within which the relevant foreign policy decisions may be made in the almost routine way that decisions on military expansion, for example, have long been made. We must, in other words, develop ways for a nation to initiate and foster a drastic change in international reality without having to accept inordinate risks of disaster.

To this end we shall need to learn of the reality images of decision makers within states as well as the reality images that can be said to underlie the policies ultimately adopted by each state, in order to be able to discover the components that create interaction over time that will contribute toward establishing different international processes and hence a new international reality.

Our recommendations, like our explanations of existing politics and interactions, will depend on growing knowledge of the determinants of reality images. We need to know not only how socialization and life experience are important, but also, at another level, how such varied factors as perceptual predispositions, the experience of "History" or "Sense of the Past," peer group relations, and personality variables such as the tendency to fantasize, the inclination to optimism or pessimism, and the tendency toward authoritarianism affect one's reality image *and* one's openness to changing his reality image.

These interests and the various others in the same rude constellation of cognitive and mental processes, tendencies, and attitudes involve all the social and behavioral sciences of man's "imaging" of reality and of ways of gaining some self-control over that "imaging." We do not yet know all we wish to know about this, but we can assemble and begin to employ enough about man's construction and creation of reality to be able to improve markedly upon much of man's present, largely unself-conscious understanding of, and wrestling with, his reality. We must do this to increase our ability to control our own reality images and then to influence others' reality images.

PART THREE

Creating a New American Foreign Policy

chapter seven

Controlling
Our Own Images

The international relations known to all of us—wars, crises, diplomatic negotiations, trade agreements—are constituted, as we have seen, by interaction processes such as military escalation and deescalation, arms races, détentes, and reciprocal exchanges. These interaction processes are constituted by the actions over time of participating states. These state actions are generally shaped by the plans and decisions (the actions) of those states' policy makers, coupled with the actions of the diplomats, soldiers, and others who carry out the agreed-upon policies.

Actions of individuals and groups, and especially the decisions of policy makers, are products of the images of reality that these men have, in particular their images of their individual responsibilities, images of their fellow decision makers, images of their state's responsibilities, images of their state's interests, images of their state's allies and adversaries, images of the international environment (geography, the structure of the international system, etc.), and images of what instruments can most promisingly be employed effectively, given these images.

Reality images, then, complex assemblies of these component images, are obviously crucial determinants of international reality. If responsible people's images of reality changed in some ways, their behavior could therefore change in ways that would significantly alter the interaction processes that occur and thereby change international reality. Thus, to develop promising ways of improving international relations we must discover not only what changes in reality images are desirable, but also what changes are possible. And to learn this we must consider first how these images arise in the mind of an individual and how individuals' images may differ.

Some Sources of Reality Images and Differences Among Them

Images of reality are often instilled by formal education, especially when they concern something not usually accessible to a child's immediate experience, such as international relations. Each of us has suffered somewhat from being educated in a conventional wisdom that was soon to change. Thus the policy makers of the years between the world wars were generally products of the isolationist-tending-toward-Idealist, and today's policy makers have come from Realist educations that, whatever their accuracies, also contained considerable inaccuracies now recognized by virtually everyone. Fortunately, the importance of formal education for human behavior seems generally limited where it concerns something which is inaccessible to experience at the time but becomes a part of experience later in life, as international reality, with wars, scares, and military drafts, often becomes.

Considerably more important is the informal education that any citizen—and especially one moving toward government service—receives "from his age." Present policy makers were educated in this sense most recently by the period of the cold war, in which all were "taught" or "trained" to look first for the lie, the deception, and the maliciousness in actions of the adversary, and hence could not be relatively "objective" in assessing proposals for political settlement, military control, or economic cooperation. The great tangle of peace hopes and fears surrounding Vietnam provides but one example of how unfortunate the consequences of this assumption, a product of our collective informal cold war education, can be. And the same thing happens in the minds of our adversaries, thereby compounding the unfortunate effects of this informal education.

Another factor even more determinant of reality images is direct experience—the raw material out of which one finally fashions, tests, and becomes convinced of the accuracy of his views about the world. It seems to be the case that too much of the same experience (such as the cold war for career diplomats, or eight years in office for Dean Rusk) produces an inability even to conceive of significant promising alternatives, let alone to examine them thoughtfully and openly. This phenomenon helps to explain why, despite the ghastly record of the uses of force in the present century—especially when it was employed "to put an end to the use of force"—the assumption that force is essential and even constructive remains unchallenged in many minds. Alternatively, as is generally granted to have been the case with Lyndon Johnson, too little experience may lead to either ignorance or timidity, each of which may force a man to rely on received conventional wisdom rather than alternative suspicions that he may develop precisely because he is *not* mentally so much the captive of this, his own more limited experience.

Such individual experience is also affected by individual cognitive processes. Psychologists and political scientists have discovered beyond much question that decision makers tend to fit incoming information into their existing theories and images, and indeed tend to perceive what they expect. Further, their interpretations of these perceptions are heavily dependent on their own images of their own state, which are heavily value-laden. This fact also helps to account for the failure of imagination in political analysis. Policy makers tend to see adversaries and their particular actions as more hostile than they are, and hence are even less likely to step back and inquire whether a given circumstance suggests the opportunity for change, or alternatively to question whether a given experience does not confirm negative assumptions about the adversary.

We also know very well that perception itself, a supposedly raw material of images, may be faulty—not necessarily because of intervening values, but simply because of noisy communication channels or mind-sets that are not open to incoming information, or a great variety of other possible impedances to accurate perception, not only by policy makers but by scholars as well.

In addition, one's images may be produced by and out of inadequate information. There was a time when most statesmen knew so little of what was going on in relations with other states—let alone about the history of international relations—that they could not be expected to be accurate analysts of international politics and foreseers of possible opportunities for significant improvement in international relations. The development and diffusion of information media today make this situation much less likely, but this by no means guarantees against particular inaccuracies or lacks. And such inaccuracies or lacks will vary among individuals and states in ways that help account for differences in reality images.

The Requirements for Controlling One's Own Images

Some of the inaccuracy of our reality images can thus be traced to particular difficulties of perception, information, and learning. Most analyses of international relations and foreign policy making therefore urge greater attentiveness and better devices for communication as the major possible improvements in foreign policy making. Undoubtedly, communication and perception can always be improved somewhat, even as individuals can be found with fewer unfortunate predispositions or greater knowledge. But such minor meliorist prescriptions have never promised the extensive improvements in policy and practice that seem necessary now. And thus, granting their (limited) usefulness, we must move beyond them to more drastic proposals.

The first stage in the development of a capacity to shape or influence the nature of international reality by increasing one's control over his own reality images is the development of *knowledge of the impact* of one's reality image upon international reality. This impact, we have seen, occurs because one's actions are shaped or informed by his image of reality, and those actions contribute to the interaction patterns that constitute international reality over time. This process of reality creation is actually much more complex, reflection will indicate, for one's action will in turn have an effect upon one's own reality image and upon others' reality images.

The first effect of action upon one's own image will likely be that of learning a behavior pattern or developing a routine in which the action is repeated, especially if the action seems successful in that it achieves the objective sought, but also (probably) if the action elicits the response the reality image predicts will occur. The latter is the normal instance in a cold war or an arms race, in which the response is not sought but is expected. And the consequence of such an experience is reinforcement of the belief or confidence in the accuracy of the reality image.

The impact of one's action upon others' reality images will similarly be one of reinforcing or challenging the image, depending upon the congruence between the expectations the image engenders and the action forthcoming. This impact of one's action upon another's image will then likely be reflected or manifest in the other's consequent action. This is the basic nature of interaction, and is exemplified in all the international relations we observe.

Knowledge or conscious recollection of this impact of one's images upon reality is hardly a sufficient instrument for the reform of international relations. But it may make possible greater self-control in otherwise provocative situations. And the greater realization of the malleable and changing nature of international reality that it encourages is an essential precondition for the next steps in gaining greater control over that reality.

The images of greatest importance here are three. First is the image of the *self*. One's own sense of identity and competence is crucial because no actor without a strong identity and self-confidence will be able to gain a significant measure of control over his own—let alone others'—images. The second image of importance is one's image of the *adversary* or enemy with whom he must deal, and whose behavior he must ultimately influence. And the third crucial image is that of the environment or the world or *international reality, including especially the instruments of effective action,* be they force, trust, or whatever. We shall examine each of these critical images and their malleability more specifically once we have determined the requisite for controlling any images.

The second stage in the development or enhancement of control over reality via control of one's images is *self-consciousness:* specific knowledge of one's own images. This knowledge of what one actually does believe about the nature of reality at a given time can be coupled with the knowledge of the impact of such reality images upon reality over time (the first condition) into a specific understanding of how existing reality is contingent upon existing reality images—how our actual reality images inform our actions and thereby contribute to the creation of reality over time through interaction. This stage, in other words, enables one to recognize and understand *one's own role* in creating the reality that we are so often tempted to assume as given and unchangeable.

The third and vital stage is the effort to become and remain self-conscious in the selection and modification of one's reality images: *self-conscious* behavior in *selection of one's reality images* in order not simply to reflect the existing conditions but to change them over time by exploiting the tendencies toward self-fulfilling and self-denying images inherent in social interaction in a given world.

Adoption of this attitude and behavior—self-conscious selection of one's reality images—is the vital way of breaking the stranglehold that our normal assumption of the existence of an independent, uncontrollable reality has had on our action. It requires accepting for practical decision and action the assumption that reality is not merely malleable but actually controllable. It thereupon denies a rather fundamental part of our common worldview, and can thereby engender considerable discomfort and even a sort of normlessness in the individual. It has, in other words, metaphysical elements or implications that run counter to much of our learned "common sense" view of the world. And because of this, it is bound to be a difficult reorientation to adopt, let alone to propagate. But in this very difficulty is the indication of its promise. Other proposals for reform avoid the difficulty by practically accepting the conventional wisdom that changes can occur only within the restrictive confines of reality as we know it, and thereupon render impossible the very reforms they propose by failing to root out the assumptions about reality that vitiate the reform proposals. Thus, this new self-conscious selection of reality images could prove as successful as it is difficult.

Ultimately, what will be required will be a fourth stage: *conscious behavior to influence others' reality images* so that their actions, rather than exploiting or vitiating our action designed to reconstruct reality, will instead couple with ours to hasten that reconstruction. This challenge cannot be approached until we have fully understood the control of our own images, and so its consideration will be postponed until the next chapter.

Some Opportunities for Control of Images: Of Self

A person who is insecure in his self-image is unlikely to operate effectively in his world. He cannot afford to take risks, which would jeopardize his already fragile sense of self, and he must also concentrate much of his effort and shape much of his action to construct and protect his underdeveloped self. These twin needs make his actions, in a time of pervasive rapid change in situations of uncertainty, both timid and inefficient.

The same difficulty can afflict a state that is unsure of itself. We well know that reasoning from the individual to the state can be inaccurate and even dangerous. The case of the individual is, however, useful as an illustration and an aid to understanding what certainly seems to be true of the state. The uncertainty and consequent lack of venturesomeness and inefficacy of both the newly created state and the self-doubting established state can be traced in significant part to this tendency.

Any state, therefore, that seeks to engineer major change in the world must begin with a strong and self-confident sense of itself. This is not to say that it must be confident of its wisdom and its manifest destiny. No state today, in our drastically changing and often seemingly uncontrolled world, seems able to maintain such confidence for long periods. And no state with the degree of technological and economic development plus political participation that are required for such effort can at the same time escape significant domestic turmoil. What it must manage to develop, then, is a tolerance for ambiguity and uncertainty—or even a welcoming of such "apparent disorder" as an opportunity for action designed to create a reordering more convenable to it—as well as a sense that its very existence or its deepest nature is not at issue unless and until its own choice to enter shared sovereignty arrangements puts these basic features at issue.

What is needed, in another formulation, is a confident zest for participating in the active reconstruction of the world. The United States certainly had such a zest following the Second World War, as its president did after 1918, and as its administration again did in 1961 until the Vietnam imbroglio and its burgeoning domestic impact began to sour its leaders and its people. There seems no necessary reason for that new dour attitude to survive the Vietnam war *if a new* and imaginative *constructive alternative to neoisolationism* is available to a people with a deep tradition of responsibility and a new sense of guilt. But the alternative of isolation and recrimination is grim.

Rather similarly, the Soviet Union, both in the years after the Second World War in which it almost single-handedly remade Eastern Europe and in the years following its great leap spaceward in 1957, has shown a zest for venturesome international participation that should survive its rupture with the People's Republic of China and lesser disappointments.

What these considerations imply is that the superstates seem possible candidates for the undertaking of international reconstruction, even though they have both suffered occasional setbacks. If opportunities and designs are available, we might hope that their military security and political interests will constitute a sufficiently strong self-image for each to be able to participate. But the sense or image of self is only one requisite.

Some Opportunities for Control of
Images: Of "The Others"

Any actor will have images of "The Others"—
the other actors with whom he interacts. To states these others
will generally appear as allies, as adversaries, and as neutrals
or nonparticipants in politics. To a superstate each of these
will be of interest, but generally only the adversaries need be
of particular concern.

Adversaries may be critically differentiated as opponents
and enemies. Any state is in competition with others, its opponents. When that competition for scarce resources (wealth,
prestige, or whatever) shifts the state's attention from attaining the mutually sought objective to preventing the other
state from attaining the objective, competition becomes conflict, an opponent becomes an enemy, and relations degenerate
dangerously.

Some competition can be transmuted, by the discovery of
new resources or a change in objectives or values, into indifference or even cooperation. Once competition becomes
conflict, however, such transmutation is almost impossible
because the participants' attention is shifted from its own
attainment objectives to its own prevention objectives. This
attention shift generally suspends the otherwise constant
assessment of the value of objectives and the reassessment
of the relative worth of somewhat incompatible objectives.
Hence a state finds itself locked in a struggle in which not
only do its motives change to defeating the other state, but
also the "basic reasons" for its desire for the disputed objective have shifted, often without this being recognized. Consider the case of the United States in Vietnam, or both the
United States and the Soviet Union in the cold war.

What is important for our effort to heighten consciousness of, and hence control over, images, is the desirability not

just of preventing competition from becoming conflict, but even more fundamentally of a state's continually reconsidering the allocation of an adversary into the category of enemy rather than opponent.

Much conventional wisdom asserts that people and social organizations such as states *need* enemies. But the apparent basis for such need is either as a spur toward unity of purpose and action—something that can be better achieved by commitment to cooperative undertaking of a new construction—or as a counter to a fractured or underdeveloped sense of self —something that can be avoided by careful development of that self-image.

In other words, the image of the others is crucial—especially the image of opponents and enemies. Where a state can refrain from emotional exacerbation and flagrant exploitation of asserted enemies for short-run purposes of psychic self-massage and unification by adversity, it will be able to exercise increasing control over its image of the enemy and thereby make possible reconsideration and perhaps reformulation of the next and most interesting image: the image of the instruments of effective action.

Some Opportunities for Control of Images: Of the Instruments of Effective Action

In our minds we see ourselves and "the others" interacting in an environment or a world, or more specifically a reality, that provides not only the occasions but also the limits and possibilities for those interactions and their outcomes. It is in analyzing relations within this environment that we attempt to reach conclusions about how we can operate effectively. As observers or students of this interaction, we seek information about the determinants of relations and of transformation of the environment or order. Comprehensive and developed views of what are the crucial determinants of the shape of and happenings in international politics are what we call, in more academic terms, theories of international politics.

Precisely where and how we get our theories of international politics is not entirely clear. Theories are developed mentally on the basis of experience—either a receiving experience in which someone tells you what he believes about what causes what, or a basically inductive experience in which you gather observations about what developments seem generally to follow the existence of certain conditions or other developments and in some way fashion these observations of temporal succession into generalizations about causality. More likely, in actual practice, a person will develop his own theory of international politics through a semiconscious combination of these two approaches.

If well-tested and confirmed theories of international politics were generally available, we could expect many individuals to have views about causality in international politics that were both sound and shared by many others—at least barring idiosyncratic lack of objectivity arising out of experience such as exile, immigration, commercial failure, or other sources of potential intellectual pathology. But unfortunately such well-tested theories of international politics—or even of its major subfields (e.g., war and crisis and international agreement) or its major components (e.g., national foreign policy making)—do not exist. Thus not only is there considerable difference among individuals concerning what causes what in international politics, but also there is rather drastic misinformation about what is known or strongly suspected about such matters, even among those who are especially interested in the field of international politics and foreign policy because they teach it, research it, or practice it.

Part of this is attributable to continuing difficulties of

communication among scholars and among practitioners, let alone between scholars and practitioners. Much more is attributable to the lack of explicit attention to theory by scholars as well as practitioners. Thus we find continuing pontification about why international politics take their present form and about how to exploit given situations from scholars and practitioners, without explicit statement of the theoretical bases on which the contentions are based. This lack is, actually, what makes the discourse pontification rather than reasoned argument. And the phenomenon can be easily observed not just in the examination of the speeches of Richard Nixon (where we would expect it because of the constraints of audience and time, if for no other reason—but also for other reasons), but also in the journal of the powerful and would-be powerful, *Foreign Affairs*, and in most international politics college textbooks.

If we paid more explicit attention to the theoretical argument implicit in most discussions of international politics we would notice two very important things. First, much of that theory is contradictory to some extent—and contradictory not in the dialectical sense for which there may be some basis, but rather in the logical sense of poor reasoning. Second, and of much greater interest to us here, we would find little reason for accepting as demonstrated, or even suggested by careful thought about our experience, much of what is tacitly offered as theory in remarks about our foreign policy and that of our cohorts.

This argument of lack of support should not be overstated, and it must be refined. As we have argued, first-glance and self-fulfilling policy have indeed offered support for many of the maxims on which we build our policy and action—especially those suggesting the significance and efficiency of force in the conduct of politics. Thus some of the discrepancy falling into this category of unsubstantiated principles applies much more to ancillary policies such as foreign aid and disarmament, on both of which our policies have been frequently much less than realistic in either the *Realpolitik* (or power-political) sense or the sense we are recommending here.

Even more important is another difficulty of most theory about international politics. It is essentially "static" in its orientation: it has been developed to account for what can be viewed as regularities in the present international situation or system, but it does not take account of fundamental changes in that system that are in fact evolving, often below the surface and seemingly invisible to those concentrating on strictly contemporary situations and problems. This is a very important part of the explanation for American failure to foresee and understand developments in relations between old allies, the Soviet Union and the People's Republic of China, just as it had been important in the failure of the great colonial powers to foresee the liberation movements sweeping much of the world at the close of the Second World War. Or the shifts in Europe precedent to that war, or to the war before it. Such failures to perceive significant systemic changes are easy to see in retrospect. The crucial challenge is to discover them while they are in progress and before they are openly manifest in a way that cannot be ignored. Much dispute between those in charge of major-power policy making and analysts recommending significant changes in those policies arises out of differential perception of system transformation. We must make major efforts to discover and project basic changes in the nature of the international system and in the major subsystems of that system—and we shall do exactly that in chapter 10.

We have already seen that the accuracy of perception of the facts or conditions at any given time can be increased through technological improvements in reconnaissance and general surveillance. Further, we can clarify and harmonize, or make logically consistent, the complex set of values we seek to obtain so that we can avoid wasting effort and defeating ourselves through the effective pursuit of reciprocally defeating objectives.

But there is an important potential danger if changes are confined to the effective improvement of our perceptions and value selections. The more effective pursuit of our present policies and implementation of our present theories of international politics will almost certainly further set back efforts to improve the international situation and reform the international system in the direction we advocate here. In other words, one of the perverse virtues of our present weaknesses in perception and valuation is that they do not, because they are often inefficient, strengthen prevailing approaches as much as they otherwise might.

In the most obvious example, the dreadful inefficiency of our approach to Vietnam has led even those who are basically strong advocates of a major American policing role around the world to object to our policy and call for reassessment of the bases of our strategy. And it has more importantly led a good many others somewhat less committed to our present objectives to suggest that we should drastically reexamine our priorities. We are already seeing that often such a reexamination on their terms leads only to either recommendations of greater efficiency or recommendations of escape into more isolationist (or Neorealist) policies. Neither of these is itself preferable to anything except our present inefficient bungling. Sheer efficiency at the service of our pernicious theory and practice of international politics would almost certainly be considerably worse. Thus it becomes imperative to pay much greater attention, not only to perception and valuation but also and more importantly to the accuracy of the theory with which we approach the world and to the possibility that the international system is presently undergoing very significant fundamental transformation. Just what opportunities for change might such examination produce?

Improved understanding of international reality would enable us to become less dominated in our thinking by the widespread view of the existing system. It is because of such mental system-domination that many otherwise imaginative, thoughtful, and concerned scholars and policy makers propose and act in ways that in fact only strengthen existing patterns of international political interaction instead of shaping the evolution of that interaction in directions less violent and more oriented toward improvement of welfare and increase of personal freedom. This claim is not as patronizing as it sounds. It simply recognizes the great difficulty any of us has in escaping from the confines of well-developed conventional wisdom—especially when we are frequently talking with those involved in contemporary crises and hence possessing time horizons effectively limited to the existing circumstances. Because men tend to imagine the future in terms of the present—generally as an extension of the present with relatively slight modifications—their efforts to be foresighted and to conceive of opportunities that might be exploited are generally less than impressive. Consequently they not only create their own reality but also contribute significantly, in their thinking as well as their action, to its maintenance. Thus we find little imaginative proposal for promising change in foreign policy and international politics despite the obvious critical need for innovation to cope with grave threats such as nuclear warfare, population expansion, and increasing political chaos in the underdeveloped states (and perhaps now in the highly developed states as well).

Further, it is particularly desirable, if not essential, to be cognizant of underlying transformations of the system while they are in process for several reasons. Most of these changes are of long-enough time horizon that the changes themselves will not drastically impede execution of a given policy at the time. But what they will tend to do is force much greater expenditure in achieving objectives in the face of long-term changes. We seek advance knowledge of these shifts because it can enable us to avoid fighting the inevitable (as some colonial powers have unsuccessfully fought the inevitable pressures for independence—for example, France in Indochina and then, somewhat surprisingly, the United States). Such knowledge can also enable us at times to encourage the desirable and discourage the undesirable within the broad range of constraints that the transformation sets (as the colonial powers might have better encouraged development of responsive— if not democratic—governments and governing groups within their colonies as they began to disengage). Both of these possibilities are manifestations of effective operation within the constrained range of possibilities brought about by fundamental transformations of the system over a longer time period. (We shall return to examination of this possibility in chapter 10 with more concrete instances arising in developments that may be discerned and foreseen now.) The opportunities will be of various depths, depending on the nature of the transformation. Thus, for example, the immediate change in international alignment involving relations between the Soviet Union and the People's Republic of China within the presently basically bipolar world offers certain limited opportunities, while the more fundamental mobilization of the Third World against the propertied major powers, a much longer-term development, presents a quite different set of constraints and occasional opportunities. Both are system transformations, one more fundamental than the other.

To foresee and understand such transformations we require much more than we do for adequate theory of the moment. Theory of the moment may be simple statements of empirical regularities or correlations: whenever certain conditions exist, we can expect a state to behave in a specified way. Such generalizations tell us what occurs when, but they do not necessarily reveal the underlying determinants of that occurrence. For the sort of systemic transformation understanding we seek, we must have as well a sense of these determinants—not just determinants of an immediate decision such as that to wage war, but those underlying determinants which create situations in which states can be enticed to wage war.

Most systemic transformation involves a change in the middle-range determinants themselves. Thus, for example, until the development of intercontinental bombers and missiles, geographical determinants were a particularly important factor in relations among widely spaced major powers. Technological change altered the significance of geography, and in fact forced us to examine both geography and technology together as a couple, or as jointly significant factors, because one enabled a state largely to overcome the impact of the other. Similarly, we shall argue later, we are presently undergoing a shift that is making attitudes of politically mobilizable populations more important than technology in determining the actions of states—a change that should transform many traditionally accepted and assumed verities about foreign policy, or at least transform the foreign policies that the verities attempt to explain and suggest. Even if the transformation does not itself inescapably alter those verities, it will offer considerable opportunities for reshaping much of international politics. We seek an understanding that will enable us to capitalize on the opportunities that transformation offers for significant change.

The Challenge of Self-Control

Differences in theories of international relations can account not only for conflicts among states but also for transformations of international relations. In most instances, the transformations of international relations have had negative effects on peace and welfare, because they have resulted from differences that produced negative processes such as arms races and escalatory hostility. We seek to develop ways of instituting and nurturing more positive processes through greater knowledge of, self-consciousness about, and conscious selection of the reality images that inform our action.

We well know that one's *image of the future* will affect the future, for that image engenders motivations, expectations, and other forces that shape actions. We know that a degree of optimism about the future (or at least the absence of the profound pessimism that seems so widespread in our time) and a longer-range perspective on the future can contribute to improved policy making in which one is at least aware of, if not actually in control of, his fate or future as it unfolds.

But this is not enough. We desperately need much greater control over our future. For this we must turn to recognition of the way in which our image of the present also affects the future by setting what we take for granted and determining what thoughts and actions will seem not only desirable but also possible. Because policy is made in the present, and because policy makers must start with that present and work from it toward an imaged future step-by-step, from today to tomorrow to the day after, and because most actions must be planned increasingly far in advance, the natural human tendency to slip into conceiving even of a contingent future world in present-day terms gives the image of the present an inordinate and often quite indefensible role in shaping the future.

But while we know we can recognize and even exploit the fact that the future depends on our image of the future, can we really exploit this recognition that the future also depends on our image of the present?

Among the major obstacles to this realization and exploitation three are of particular importance. First, there is a sub-structure of inertial factors. The initial factor is institutions (political, economic, social, communications, etc.) that are often well harmonized with the dominant worldview, whether as cause or as effect, and may therefore tend to dissuade initiative, education, and even imagination. Some theorists, following Marx, believe these institutions so dominant that they cannot be overcome until "their time has come"; other theorists, following hints in Marx and examples in Lenin and his subsequents, believe that consciousness can be induced and can prevail. The latter seems the sensible presumption, at least when the alternative of resigned inaction in a time of troubles is considered. But we must remember the likely iner-tial effect of some institutions, and our course must be de-signed to combat this where it is likely to be strong.

The second inertial factor is the existence of worldviews that are more comprehensive than the one we are developing as an alternative. This is an almost inevitable obstacle for any truly novel departure because the predominant worldview has both age and the support of institutions as advantages. Its disadvantage and potentially fatal weakness, beyond any inherent contradictions that may emerge, is its record of rela-tive failure. The degree of that failure may vary, of course. But just as things *could* always have been worse (and thus a worldview might be deemed effective and hence accurate), so things *could* always have been better (and thus no worldview will ever seem wholly accurate).

The third inertial factor is the existence in man of a cog-nitive tendency toward completeness, coherence, or consist-ency in one's symbolic system. This tendency is the context in which small changes in reality image produce cognitive dissonance that tends to drive the individual toward recidi-vistic consistency—rejection of the novelty that is inconsistent with the rest of his image. This tendency seems to be a major reason for the failure of so many efforts at gradual, piecemeal change in education and in societal engineering. Its existence and pervasive operation argues mightily for fundamental analysis and comprehensive change.

An analogous phenomenon at the social level constitutes the second major possible obstacle to self-control of reality images. In social relations, peer pressure toward conformity is a pervasive phenomenon. This becomes important because both policy making and analysis are increasingly collegial, or group, activities. This means it is of growing importance that the relevant group—certainly the policy bureaucracy and perhaps even the attentive or active public—be involved in the changing consciousness so that it does not tend to elicit recidivistic conformity from the fractional elite that has achieved greater understanding and is attempting to develop and employ it. It may always be that a kind of gentle deception similar to that practiced in the name of "need to know" restrictions and claims of "executive privilege" will help to protect the innovator from these pressures. But there is no guarantee that they will, and further there can be no certainty that the innovative element will be adequate to its task even conceptually, let alone administratively, without the assistance and the criticism of others who may nonetheless tend toward recidivism.

This difficult problem may further be compounded indirectly by the likely weakness of the innovator himself precisely because he is in a sense engaged in a form of self-deception. For he must acclimate himself to conceiving of the present reality not in positivist terms as something existing concretely at the given time, but rather as something constantly in the course of "becoming," of coming into existence and in its turn carrying the seeds of what will succeed it. And this image of the nature of present reality is foreign enough to his learned sense of the present as instantaneous and static and to his sensory experience that he must in some sense continually "deceive" himself into accepting it to avoid letting his immediate sensory inclinations deceive him much more fundamentally. Needless to say, this is a requirement that makes him all the more vulnerable to peer pressures toward recidivistic conformity with others less conscious.

The third major obstacle extends this difficulty over time. Because people themselves change and because the people in positions of responsibility change over time, any effort at reconstruction requires some kind of commitment—one that binds both oneself and one's subsequents—not inordinately and beyond the sufficient testing of the innovation, but sufficiently to overcome the effect of the delay in the payoff of the innovation beyond a time when popular misunderstanding and discontent may tend to interfere.

Commitment is also essential to the effort to influence the adversary's reality image and action. No invitation to him to desert his present ways for a novel departure is likely to be attractive if he cannot be confident of one's continued participation. And no effort to influence him by example will likely be convincing if it is short-lived or wildly fluctuating.

It will not ultimately suffice simply to control one's own image of reality and act accordingly. The processes that are constituted by reality image-informed national actions are interaction processes. And the likelihood of successfully eliciting the desired reconstructive behavior from a quite conflicted adversary without also over time influencing his reality image seems slight. One's actions must be designed to entice and reassure. And thus one's reality image must be designed in part to incorporate carefully engineered influence over the other's reality image.

chapter eight
Influencing
Others' Images

The actions and the underlying image of reality of another state are essentially products of the same basic factors that shape our image and action. The perspective from which image and action emerge is necessarily different because the other state has a different position and a different biography or history. It differs also in that the assortment of states that the other state observes and includes in its image of the world includes us as an actual or potential adversary, in the way that ours includes it.

This obvious fact—that our image of other states includes it but not us, while its includes us but not itself—provides a potential opportunity for changing international relations that we cannot afford to ignore.

We have found that—despite significant changes in the number and alignment of states in world politics; despite drastic developments in the technologies of transportation, destruction, and information; despite major changes in economic relations and multinational institutions—the nature of international relations has remained relatively constant. International relations still are dominated by the application of force and threat of force, and the welfare of people seems often the first casualty in this victory of force over all other possible contenders as arbiter of interstate relations. This is the situation with which we are confronted, and it is from this situation that we must move.

We have argued that a major factor in this continuity of the nature of international relations in the face of drastic changes in so many of its elements is the continued unquestioning acceptance of conventional notions of what the instruments of effective action are. The dominance of force is traceable to the pervasive belief in its efficacy—at least its superior efficacy relative to recognized alternatives. Over and over again, reliance on the use of force creates patterns of interaction that vitiate the efforts of each side in a conflict to achieve its objectives and, more often than not, to maintain the minimal possessions and favorable conditions with which it entered the contest. These international processes of escalation in mistrust, hostility, destruction, and pernicious learning are created in large part by the reciprocal resort to force, and in turn strengthen the desperation with which that resort is pursued.

Obviously, something should be done to stop this. But no state has yet accepted an analysis of this process of international political disintegration fundamental and incisive enough to enable and even compel it to develop a genuinely new approach to its foreign policy and thereby to international politics.

Even where long-standing arguments have been internally compelling—as, for example, arguments against arms races and for disarmament, or against the untimely perpetuation of the cold war—no party has been able to see its way clear to a comprehensive program of significant unilateral measures designed to initiate such progress, because it has not believed the other party or parties trustworthy enough to allow it to risk departing from the ongoing pattern of interactive confrontation.

The response most concerned analysts and advocates

have made to this "prisoner's dilemma" situation has been to attempt to design limited unilateral measures in slowly progressive sequences that are, if not foolproof, at least quickly reversible if the adversary does not respond constructively. A program of carefully designed and sequenced measures is surely essential if progress is to be made. But the great difficulty to be overcome is the tendency for the ancillary protective measures and the defensive mechanisms incorporated in the initiatives and occasional agreements to outweigh and undermine the measures themselves by their emphasis upon traditional conceptions of and criteria for "security."

The case of the limited nuclear test-ban treaty is instructive. It was designed primarily to prohibit atmospheric testing because that was both dangerous to health and a major component in the arms race of the 1950s and early 1960s. But in order to reassure those who believed that the other side was untrustworthy and that nuclear testing was essential to security, provision was made in the treaty for unilateral renunciation on short notice. And the president, in attempting to gain the support of hostile military and political figures, pledged that we would drastically increase our underground testing program. The result has been that we have tested even more than we did before the agreement. The nuclear arms race has actually accelerated and international tensions seem not to have been significantly reduced over time by the agreement. We can be pleased that the atmosphere is less regularly polluted by nuclear testing. But that is little comfort to those anxiously seeking a significant improvement in the nature of international relations.

The chief problem here is that most such measures as the test ban begin by accepting the necessity and even the promise of military weaponry as the guarantor of world peace and welfare. This tacit acceptance speaks louder than the actions taken to curtail the raciness of weapons procurement, and the only real change, if any there be, is a marginal decrease in the likelihood of pernicious side effects of the militarization of relations—a change that may unfortunately lessen our vigilance against and our fear of the almost inescapable exacerbation of relations by the mutual deployment of bigger and better arsenals.

Thus, if we are to achieve any significant change in the nature of international relations, we must begin by recognizing the need to penetrate to the assumptions about the essentiality and even efficacy of the reliance on force. And we must build upon the fact of the widespread, almost universal, unquestioning acceptance of these assumptions.

We have already considered the conscious alteration of *our* image of reality—and particularly its emphasis upon the efficacy of force—and found that a better understanding of the nature and operation of international processes provided justification for such a change. But the long-term impact of such a change will be dependent in large part on the eventual acquiescence or enthusiastic agreement of others who could otherwise act in ways virtually certain to reawaken the primordial fears and conventional wisdom that presently inform our foreign policy and that of the others.

Our Actions and Others' Images

Inevitably, our actions and our statements about world affairs, which are the perceivable indicators of our analysis and our intentions, will influence the images of our adversaries. If we change our own image and thereupon our action, we will be changing a major input into the images and actions of others. This change may escape notice for a while because of the proclivity to see what one expects to see, and even when it is seen it may not be immediately convincing because of the predisposition to expect malevolence and treachery that defines not only the cold war but even traditional twentieth-century international relations.

But the prospect for long-term success is not as bleak as this might seem to imply—partly because of the impact of international processes and partly because of the impact of changed consciousness. Any action by any party to interaction will affect that interaction. The sorts of actions that an innovating state attempting to reconstruct international relations will take are bound to create obstacles to the continuation of processes of hostility and armament and escalation, and eventually even to set in motion counterprocesses, even if the adversaries are suspicious and the indifferents are abstemious. We shall examine this impact further in the next chapter, which is devoted to affecting and controlling international processes.

At the moment, we must examine further the impact upon consciousness. Any state attempting to innovate in the ways we advocate will have a splendid opportunity to educate as it acts. If it does not speak eloquently and incisively about its activity, it will almost certainly delay the impact of the actions upon the adversary's understanding of international reality—its consciousness. If it does speak, it can make two important sets of claims. The first is about its own intentions and interests—a traditional topic for state pronouncement, but one which would be substantially novel in its content, and might well be the more compelling because of the actions taken which the words are designed to explain.

The more important set of claims, however, will be its explanation for its changed course of action—an explanation in terms of its new or more highly developed understanding of the process of international reality creation. Such an explanation could be quite compelling in itself. But even if the other states did not find it compelling, they would at least find it peculiar enough that they could not dismiss it as more militant or liberal rhetoric. Thus its strangeness alone would encourage more careful attention by others, and its assertions should merit and repay that attention.

But explanation as such may not suffice, even coupled with innovative action. While the continuities in international relations over the long run are overwhelming to the analyst, the instantaneous discontinuities often overwhelm the policy maker. Thus *commitment* will be a crucial factor. Commitment can be understood as an actor's placing himself in a position such that he will be required to act in a specified way even when on the merits of the situation he does not wish to. This is what makes commitments so important in international relations: they compel an actor to act against his felt immediate interests, should those felt interests change.

The ability of a state to commit itself in advance to adhering to a program of international political reconstruction will be crucial for two reasons. First, an adversary—and even an ally—will be inclined to doubt, if not the sincerity at the time, then at least the constancy over time, of a state venturing such a new departure. This doubt will arise partly because conventional wisdom will deny the wisdom as well as the efficacy of the effort, and partly because the program and even its progenitors will be seen as reversible or replaceable by other actors conscious of their own difficulties in engineering and maintaining initiatives, and even in remaining in office.

Second, the ability of the initiating state to commit itself will be essential as well because these suspicions of others may well otherwise prove to be well founded. The difficulties, the momentary setbacks, the temptations of political adversaries to exploit popular disquiet over major innovation—all these likely elements in the development of relations once the effort is being undertaken can become threats to its continuation.

Some of the difficulty should be avoidable through popular education, which should be easier in this country than it would in others not merely because our communications media are so much better developed than those of other states, but even more so because we have always been a people desirous of constructive innovation and moral contribution to international relations. Our biggest disasters as well as our greatest successes can be traced in substantial measure to this would-be beneficent interest. Some argue that our experience in Vietnam will fundamentally weaken or even destroy this desire. But it seems more likely that Vietnam will produce a temporary dormancy in our desires that will if anything result in their revivification and strengthening. The growing desire for atonement could be dangerously exploited. Only the coming of a new and constructive program offers real promise.

Our program must, in other words, both entice and reassure our own citizens, just as our actions and words must entice and reassure our fellow states. The other states must be convinced of our sincerity and our commitment to this new interactive involvement, as well as of our interests and our strength in seeking them. These will be the critical elements in others' images of us, and those images will inform their reactions to our efforts over time.

As others' adversary, we can and indeed must act to do four critical things. First, we must convince an adversary of our peaceable intentions. Such efforts are a traditional element of the foreign policy of even the most belligerent states. Hence the great credibility problem any state, except a wholly unarmed state, must have. The conventional way of convincing another of one's pacific desires is, paradoxically, to show commitment plus firmness. We certainly must improve on that. Embarking upon the other tasks may help considerably.

The second task is to inform other states of opportunities for improvements of relations that result immediately from this new understanding of the processes of reality creation in international politics—opportunities for everything from much more arms control and much less cold warring, to the fourth task (see below).

The third task is to inform others of the available or inventable alternative images of world order. Conventional wisdom recognizes the balance-of-power image of order in which all states shift alignments when any state threatens to dominate. This "order" has resulted in the wars we all know and few love. Conventional wisdom also recognizes the empire image of order in which one state polices the others, as Rome and perhaps Britain once did, and as it sometimes seems the United States has attempted recently. And conventional wisdom recognizes the collective-security image of order that is supposed to be the essence of international organization to prevent war; but wisdom has it that this approach never works, and certainly it has not yet done so effectively.

But other images can be developed and could be employed, some deriving from efforts to cope with the cultural bases of differences among peoples and states; others from new understandings of human nature, needs, and desires; and still others derivable from Asian principles of organization by hierarchy rather than by boundary—to mention but a few.

And this raises the fourth—and perhaps the most important—task of the innovative state: encouraging the cooperation of other states and other peoples in the development and elaboration of other models or images of world order.

These images of world order will come to play a major part in the images of the future held by reconstructing states and hopefully in those of other states too. They will inevitably open possibilities that will begin to inform thinking in the present. And by this process they will become possibilities to be considered by states and other actors seeking to develop a new world order. That task must and will be pursued, we have argued, once states have come to understand better the process of reality creation, through the gaining of greater control over international processes.

chapter nine
Controlling and Exploiting International Processes

Arms races, cold wars, détentes, and other extended phenomena so characteristic of international relations as we know them are constituted over time by processes of reaction, interpretation, integration, misunderstanding, and the like. These processes are constituted by patterns of action-and-reaction that are made up of actions by the states involved.

A state seeking to alter the nature of international relations has only two basic tools or elements to work with: its own actions, and its understanding of the dynamics of international relations. What then can it actually do?

At the level of interaction processes, we now know enough about the reaction processes underlying arms race, escalation in wartime, and hostility in "cold wars" to attempt to shape our policies to avoid them. But this can only be done, if indeed it can be done at all, if we are able to shift our prime emphasis *at the level of policy* from particular stakes (such as holding or defending a piece of territory) to the tenor of international relations (reducing the degree of violence, for example). If so, we can then reestablish the dominance of policy over program so that the inevitable process-generation of programmatic pursuit of a stake can be countered—even perhaps at the cost of abandonment of stakes at various times and in various places.

Such abandonment, as we know from discussions of Indochina and previously of South Korea, Taiwan, etc., is never easy and indeed seems impossible in America *if* it is seen as surrender or defeat. But such a view might be avoided if it is seen as a programmatic pursuit of a specific process goal such as lessening international violence or armed confrontation, or increasing self-determination. When it is so conceived, emphasis must be put on the dynamic of the process—the "multiplier effect" that any such move, if it is well designed, is likely to have. Otherwise, the immediate cost will almost always seem prohibitive, even though the eventual cost of retention will probably prove exorbitant. This is an important provision at the level of the policies we insert into interaction in the world. This self-consciousness and usually explicit statement will be particularly important precisely because the Soviet Union shows every sign of being entangled in the same short-visioned concentration on stakes rather than processes.

The fact that both superpowers are so enmeshed provides the greater superficial reciprocal confirmation of the conventional wisdom on each side about international politics, as we have seen. For each acts in ways that confirm the other's image of aggressive hostility, and this is then seen by policy makers and scholars alike, on each side, as confirmation of their beliefs about the reality of the other's intentions. Thus each acts in ways that create and intensify negative processes in international relations.

For this reason, if one party is to attempt to break this spiral, he must be especially explicit about the rationale for what he is doing in order to help reeducate the other *and* in order to remain steadfast himself despite the inevitable difficulties, especially in terms of particular stakes, as well as in America explicitly for the education of the concerned public.

The Elements of Interaction

But before a comprehensive policy of this sort can be developed, we must increase recognition of the building blocks of international processes: the instruments of effective action and the types of interaction they can create. The fundamental elements employed are words, goods, deeds, and weapons. The basic types of interaction in which we will be particularly interested are discussion, exchange, and coercion.

In discussion, words are employed as information or arguments to affect the beliefs of another state or its actors, In exchange, goods or deeds or both are traded by two or more parties in a combination that each party finds beneficial. In coercion, goods and weapons are used to alter behavior more directly.

When discussion conveys information about one party's intentions which are conditional upon the reaction of the other, it incorporates threats and promises. A threat is a statement that one will do, in a contingency, something that he would obviously prefer not to do. The basic types of threat are the deterrent ("If you do something that I don't want, I'll do something that you don't want"), the desistent ("Stop doing something that I don't want, or I'll do something that you don't want"), and the compellent ("Do something that I want, or I'll do something that you don't want"). The deterrent threat is recognizably common in international relations. The desistent threat is less so because its credibility is lessened by the fact that the adversary has thus far acted undesirably with impunity. The compellent threat is even more difficult because the only way one can become credibly committed to it is to begin administering punishment until the other party acts. America's failure in the Vietnam war can be analyzed at this level largely in terms of its effort to use the desistent threat in Vietnam and the compellent threat in Paris and Hanoi.

Threats succeed or fail as they are responded to. As social scientist Kenneth Boulding has indicated, there are four possible responses to a threat: submission, defiance, counterthreat, and integration. Submission results in agreement on the terms of the threatener, as in surrender and appeasement. Defiance creates a state of conflict if the threatener then executes his threat. Counterthreat ("If you do something that I don't want, I'll do something that you don't want") creates a situation of deterrence if it works.

Integration as a response to threat transcends the level of the immediate conflict by moving to a higher level of commonality, of images of common values and interests, as happens often in race relations and marriage, sometimes in alliances, and occasionally in international organizations such as the United Nations. But of course rather than integration, disintegration may well occur, and indeed is probably the more likely eventuation from threat interactions, as it is from coercion interactions.

But not so from promises, the other fundamental instrument used in discussion. The crucial difference between a threat and a promise is that the threatener gets what he wants *or else* he gives, while the promiser gives *only if* he gets. In international relations, the threat has an "advantage" in that we find and assume divergent interests among states, so the threat's credibility is more easily established. The promiser must create or nourish trust in him by the adversary if he is to succeed. If it were not for the pervasive, although often invisible, positive interdependence that underlies relations among states, promises could not succeed. But neither could threats succeed without at least the negative interdependence or mutual vulnerability by now so characteristic of international relations.

Exchange interactions, in which goods and/or behavior are traded, are primarily cooperative, but they have crucial elements of competition in the setting of the terms of trade. Coercion interactions, on the other hand, are basically conflictual, but include cooperative setting of limits to the range of the conflict and the extent of the harm done.

In each case, the response to a particular instigation or reaction determines whether the cooperation or the conflict expands, contracts, or remains constant. Expansion (as in escalation of military interaction or intensification of arms races or increase in cooperation) will tend to create the multiplier effect that encourages integration or disintegration, and the same will be true of the less frequent contraction (as in deescalation of warfare, isolationist curtailment of foreign involvement, or disarmament). But our analysis requires categories of interaction less pure, less abstract.

The Types of Interaction

For our purposes in understanding the components out of which international reality is and may be constructed, we will find it helpful to employ four categories of interaction.

1. The first is the *responsive* relation in which each party acts in a way that replicates, or repeats identically, the action of the other. We are most familiar with this type in phenomena such as arms races, aggressive action in wartime, and non-security competition such as the space race, the education-of-scientists race, and other instances having primarily good effects in terms of development or other internal objectives. What is common to each of these types of relation is the matching of an action by one party with a similar action by the other. In some cases this will take place in a measured way of controlled increases in expenditure or other effort, but often there proves to be a dynamic which produces the "race" effect.

2. The second type of relation is often termed *bargaining* and involves the trade of something by one party to the other

for something it desires. Phenomena such as international trade are clear cases of bargaining, but so are such things as limitation of types of aggressive action in wartime. What will be characteristic of all such instances is that one party will be trading something that he values somewhat (otherwise he would probably have "discarded" it; the value might, of course, derive simply from the fact that the other party, a competitor, desires it) to another party for something he desires more than his present possession. And the same in reverse must of course be true of the other party.

3. The third type of relation is a unilateral action which is exploited by the other party. This *unilateral/exploited* relation can be found in cases of self-sacrifice—rather rare in international relations but not so unusual in interpersonal relations among members of a family or close friends, for example. Its chief manifestation in international relations, more argued and proposed than observed, is security initiatives such as cuts in one's military budget or stockpile of fissionable materials or arsenal designed or hoped to encourage an adversary to do likewise and hence improve the condition of both by lessening the danger of accidental war or war via arms race. If such an initiative is replicated by the other party, the case becomes one of responsive interaction. The exploitation response, in which the other party takes advantage of such a gentle gesture, is believed by the conventional wisdom to occur much more often, partly because the stated motives of a nation generally considered hostile are disbelieved; and partly because the promise of further good to accrue to both parties following replication is doubted, and hence the opportunity for immediate gain via exploitation is taken.

4. The final basic type of relation, by our categorization, is the unilateral action that is ignored by the adversary—neither replicated nor exploited. This *unilateral/ignored* interaction occurs very frequently but usually without the notice

of the students of world politics, because it is generally suspected that anything one state does that another does not somehow respond to must be either a mistake or irrelevant to the development of international relations. Among the many examples of such actions are cultural ventures and much nonsecurity action such as foreign assistance. Even more extremely, one could put many internal actions designed to improve the capabilities of the state for science and engineering or public health in this category, for most of them are not emulated by other states as they might be.

Employing This Analysis

This particular categorization of relations among two states should enable us better to analyze and understand the security impact of patterns of relations among the United States and its adversaries, whether they be the Soviet Union, the People's Republic of China, Cuba, or any other state.

The immediate challenge to the United States or any other initiating state, should it wish to improve the nature of international relations of which it is a part, is to transfer subject areas (such as military buildups, space programs, or military assistance abroad) from the first category of replicated or responsive interactions to the second or bargaining category, where, for example, military buildup may be treated as an instance of national action subject to bargaining with the adversary. This transfer is the first essential step in the achievement of arms control measures—measures agreed upon by two competing military powers to reduce or otherwise constrain their military holdings or postures so that neither party loses security. At the same time, neither party need lavishly spend its precious resources in ways bound to be emulated by the other and hence rendered ineffective, with the added likelihood that they will increase the insecurity of both. The immediate challenge, then, is to shift such aggressive or otherwise militant activities from the realm of those matters assumed to call automatically for replication by the other party to the realm of matters to be negotiated over and settled in a bargaining approach.

Such a shift is easy to analyze and easy to recommend— and occasionally relatively easy to achieve—as the limited nuclear test ban was suddenly achieved in the summer of 1963 following the coming of political conditions conducive to it. But such a shift is generally not easily approached. The effective approach is unlikely to be through everyone suddenly deciding to be reasonable and to reason together. Rather it will probably be through a diverse collection of acts that could fall in the third category—unilateral and exploitable—but are very carefully designed so that if they fail to induce the appropriate replicative response they will fall into the fourth category of ignored initiatives, rather than being seriously exploited. Thus, for example, if the United States undertakes to move the military budget from the category of those items explosively increased to that of those subject to negotiation and hence to control, it may choose to attempt this by undertaking a pronounced unilateral cutback in spending of a certain sort and inviting the adversary to replicate. This could be an action in the third category—open to exploitation by the adversary—should he be untrusting or doubtful or malicious. The requirement is that it be designed so that he is likely to be confident, and so that, should it fail to induce reciprocation, the adversary will be less tempted to respond exploitatively and more inclined simply to let it pass or to ignore it.

This is quite a set of specifications for the design of innovative pieces of foreign and military policy. The specifications are not novel, but their organization and emphasis will be, if they are derived from an analysis of types of interaction rather than simply from the perspective of a state attempting to get its way in international politics.

Applying This Knowledge

Designing a foreign policy while conscious not only of the state's objectives, but also of the critical considerations we have been developing here, will be more difficult and more demanding than it generally is today. It will require recognition and avoidance of such tendencies as that for state objectives to become transmogrified into largely territorial and institutional objectives rather than environmental or process objectives. It will require conscious analysis of both international interaction and policy proposals in terms of the constituent instruments of effective action and types of interaction so that we can improve our understanding of how international reality is being shaped over time and might be reconstructed by our policies. And it will require frequent resort to our own conscious images of that reality and attention to those of other states so that we can find and control the roots of the processes that emerge from these images to shape reality over time.

We have already examined in chapter 5 some major processes inherent in policy making, including distortion of perception and of communication, decision process domination of substantive considerations, objective or goal rigidification, bureaucratic politicking, routinization of action, and support processes such as the bandwagon and underdog effects. We have also examined similar processes as they are inherent in policy execution, such as misunderstanding, routinization, and reaction processes. Controlling these processes is in substantial part a matter of remaining conscious of their ever-presence as tendencies and so acting to override them by conscious design. That design capability will benefit considerably from increased individual and bureaucratic learning over time as consciousness continues and is heightened by greater insight and diffused by example and instruction.

Particular objectives and policies designed to achieve them will require particular controls on such processes. This requirement will derive partly from the nature of the objective and policy, and partly from the trending environment within which it is sought. Thus, before we attempt to specify further some basic measures and policies that might promise the improvements in international relations that we recommend, it is important to examine the present for indicators of emergent trends, some of which may be encouraging and hence exploitable, and others of which may be threatening and hence candidates for control.

PART FOUR

Creating a New World Politics

chapter ten
The Contextual Trends

Any effort to forecast major significant developments in the coming decade or two is in essence a risky activity. Neither our predictive methodology nor our theory of international politics is adequate to offer the forecaster the confidence he would like. Any forecast should be taken with caution if at all. Nonetheless, thinking about the future is increasingly important—especially if we are discontented enough with our present to wonder whether the reasons for our discontent are likely to persist and what the opportunities for reshaping the dimensions of our future in our future might be. Thus, we shall attempt, with some trepidation and appropriate warning, to suggest what seem the most likely general outlines of the more distant future of the international system—the context within which we will make or break our chances for survival and contentment, not only in our relations with other states but also in our coping with our primarily internal problems.

The Tendencies of Most Forecasts

Most efforts to forecast the future of international politics concentrate their primary attention on the patterns of the international system itself. This view implies a theory of international politics that asserts that major happenings are determined primarily by the nature of the system, rather than, say, by the qualities of the leadership of key countries, by developments within the politics of key countries, or by the economies of key countries. There is still, as we well know, considerable dispute about which of these possible determinants is actually the most important determinant of what happens in international politics—if indeed it be any of these.

Most efforts to account for the nature of international politics today focus on several key factors: (1) the technological development that has produced a revolution in weaponry, making major war highly undesirable if not impossible in ways and to extents not previously true; (2) the proliferation of newly independent and politically and economically unstable states that tend to quarrel with their neighbors and provide temptations for intervention by the major powers despite the technological deterrents to such interventions; and (3) the ideological quarrel, first between the two superpowers and subsidiarily between each superpower and its major ally or allies over the desirable shape of society and who should be allowed to determine it, which provides both the incentive to intervene in small-state quarrels and the basis for continuing confrontation between the superpowers and their socio-economic-political systems. Put another way, ideology is generally argued to provide the motivation, technology the means and their now intrinsic limitations, and political independence and instability in the Third World the occasion, for big-power contest. These three key factors and their specific states or conditions are rarely fashioned into a careful theory of international politics and the foreign policies that constitute the politics. Nonetheless, they do, even in the crude form offered, seem to enable many to understand major happenings better.

But do they enable us to foresee major new developments in international politics? Not very well, at least as generally formulated. The easiest way to forecast is to seek apparent trends and then extrapolate them. Thus we might expect continued technological developments in weaponry—or more precisely in the technologies of transportation (missiles and other delivery systems) and destruction (nuclear and other weaponry) that would make major war even less attractive, and thereby shift attention even further toward unconventional and especially guerrilla warfare (which might in its turn be subject to increasing technological development such as chemical weaponry and novel detection devices). We might expect either increasing stability or increasing instability in the newer states, depending on what we viewed as prime determinants of stability; and in consequence we might expect greater or fewer temptations to intervention by the major powers. Finally, we might anticipate that the ideological disputes among the superpowers would subside as the challenges from allies (especially the People's Republic of China and a resurgent Western Europe) increase and as American and Soviet society tend to "converge" in nature.

Each of these general forecasts has been widely made. But none of them seeks to offer convincing argument, nor do the three seem clearly to converge on a picture of the future of world politics that is convincing beyond a suggestion that conflicts may become more regional and less conventional and that the roles of the superpowers may decline somewhat. Worst of all, however, none of these projective forecasts enables us to perceive or anticipate any major changes of the sort that each of these three factors produced at the close of the Second World War. In other words, projecting the developments of the years between the world wars would not have led most analysts to foresee any of these three major developments: (1) nuclear power and rocketry were not only unknown but generally unconceived; (2) the great movement for colonial independence was generally unanticipated; and (3) the drastic restructuring of international politics in which the major adversaries would realign so that instead of a capitalist democratic and communist totalitarian alliance against fascism we would face a capitalist-communist confrontation with the formerly fascist states generally on the capitalist side. None of these major transforming factors which we now generally cite as the key determinants of contemporary international politics would have been foreseen by conventional projective efforts at forecasting immediately prior to their emergence.

Such recent weakness in forecasting should not only give us pause about any effort at forecasting, but even more should lead us to look elsewhere than supposedly "obvious" and projectable trends for the major determinants of drastic change. This does not in itself demonstrate that there will indeed be drastic change, but the record of the twentieth century certainly suggests the likelihood of such drastic change. What we must do, then, is seek possible sources of significant transformations in the circumstances within which nations (should they survive as we know them) will be making major policy, and even more important possible sources of the values or objectives that policy makers will most likely be attempting to achieve. This is what we shall suggest here.

It would be a major error to ignore nations other than the United States and the Soviet Union in attempting to project major developments. But the most manageable approach —and that most relevant to our analysis and recommendations concerning American foreign policy—is to examine the likely developments in American and Soviet interests and situations before considering other states.

A Speculative Forecast of Critical Possibilities

Although we can expect technological development in weaponry to continue unabated, barring drastic arms control arrangements that seem unlikely, ultimately the most significant technological development—excluding only possibly nuclear weaponry—has already largely occurred and has gone almost entirely unappreciated. It is the development and widespread proliferation of cheap effective media of information transmission, such as the transistor radio and increasingly television. It was long thought that such development would serve the interests of the establishment, enabling them to spread their word to all concerned. But its most crucial effect has been the virtual opposite: breaking the previous governmental or system monopoly on information by enabling foreign sources (such as the Voice of America, Radio Moscow, Radio Peking, depending on locale, and the "underground" or "pirate" stations increasingly prevalent all over the world) whose orientation is not system-dominated, to broadcast information that differs from the prevailing view and entertainment that diverges from prevailing standards. Further, even the establishment broadcasters have not foreseen the divergent effects of information on their own audiences. Too much of the combination of varying governmental assertions, whether or not they are contrasted with other accounts, has led to and exacerbated development of "credibility gaps" between government and its subjects, which of course jeopardizes the authority of governmental and perhaps other institutions. But what seems most important here is the differential impact of the normal (including system line or party line) and the abnormal that creeps in unnoticed even in carefully tailored newscasts and speeches. It is striking how Kremlinologists, for example, have become able to read the broadcasts of the Soviet hierarchy effectively, and even more how those inside the Soviet Union have become able to do so. Thus the populace—the attentive because significantly discontented populace—is able to gain information not just from foreign sources but also from domestic sources.

But what is most important here is not the particular information received—much if not most of which is inevitably erroneous—but the opening of several possibilities and the consequent requirement that the listener attempt to discriminate and seek other sources for confirmation, whether those sources be American jazz and rock music in the Soviet Union or antiestablishment "underground" newspapers in the United States. The shared experience of living in an official orthodoxy with an antiofficial underground may prove especially important in shaping the attitudes and the openness of emergent leaders who have had this experience in an increasingly industrialized and bureaucratized society—whether that society be the Soviet Union or the United States.

This possibility shifts our attention from information media and their messages to the more conscious consideration of values. The present generation of leadership in both the United States and the Soviet Union was socialized in the years of mutual xenophobia. In the Soviet Union this was the era of "capitalist encirclement" and internal purges that turned much of the country into a foreign land to be feared for the threat it posed to the politically unorthodox. In the United States the reaction toward isolation following the First World War, compounded by the depression that first arose abroad, led to greater protection economically and politically and was capped by a surprise embroilment in a foreign and almost universal war. It is hardly surprising that these elites should have become and remained opposed not only to the strange from abroad, but also to the unorthodox at home. In a sense, the very fact that the two leaderships are finally able to consider accommodations with adversaries—if primarily out of desperation born of thermonuclear threat—is itself a remarkable tribute to the adjustability of the individual, even in his middle age. Nonetheless, these leaderships have clearly not yet been able to revise their attitudes and redirect their actions sufficiently to engineer the major reconstruction of international politics that alone offers some hope of allowing achievement of the wishes of the alert and imaginative for conciliation across borders and drastic humane reconstruction at home.

These desires are not popular with the authorities in either country, partly because they imply renunciation of the major principles on which their lives and their policies have been based, and partly because these very principles suggest that their youthful attitudes are instances of bewitchment by interests hostile not simply to the leaders but to the material structures they have built to enshrine their ideals. It is these understandable fears that lead to efforts in both countries to characterize divergent attitudes as subversive and inspired from abroad.

In an important sense they are indeed subversive—but not in the sense that is believed by the leadership. They are not, of course, fostered and peddled from abroad. Rather, they result from the relatively independent analysis of those not imprisoned by the collective consciousness of their respectable and responsible elders. But their subversiveness does not even extend to the respective socioeconomic-political systems themselves. Most American leaders are afraid that these attitudes of conciliation and altruism in the leadership of the young will spell the doom of the relatively free enterprise economic system which we term capitalism and the political system of allegedly beneficent rule by somewhat responsible elites which we term democracy. This belief arises primarily out of the acceptance of two fallacious principles. Economically, the argument is based on the assumption of eternal scarcity coupled with unlimited wants. The accurate point, however, is that both scarcity and the believed unlimitedness of material wants are proving less extensive than was believed by the "children" and adolescents of the depression. This is a point that many of the young understand almost intuitively and hence do not worry about. It would be hard to find much sympathy for abolition of initiative capitalism if this system proves willing to minister to the needs of its disadvantaged, and it is efforts to prove this that occupy so much of the time of the young elites.

The same sort of phenomenon holds politically, although it too is not realized by the present political elite. Those in power realize quite well that they hold power because the system is structured to favor certain elites, and they fear that the emphasis upon "participatory democracy" by the most vocal youth is an effort to destroy the principle of rule by elites and thereby create chaos. This is not, however, the case with most of the youth. The principle of elite rule is not just a natural human development in large-scale social organization, but indeed the logical extension of that favorite dictum of the young, "do your own thing." The point the young seem to want most to make is that authority structures must be more responsive to the interests of those who are not in the ruling elite—that it must become both responsive and anticipatory while engaging less in "brainwashing." This is the major reason why the frequent chortling by the elders that the larger percentage of the youth are neither active nor interested in the political programs of the youth elite so badly misses the point: all it has ever taken, and all it will ever take, to bring about significant change is a broadly interested (alternatively, a well-armed) elite that will accede to power with attitudes significantly divergent from those of the previous rulers, and attempt to restructure the key aspects of the system so that it will become closer to its constituents and less the tool of vested minority interests.

In this sense, much of the resistance by the ruling elites is sensible: if the young have their way, the interests will certainly have decreasing percentages of control and probably less of the wealth that this control allows. On the other hand, the fear that they will simply be stripped of their possessions in a vast reallocation of existing resources is foolish. What increasing numbers of the young understand much better than their elders is that scarcity, however pervasive it presently may be, is no longer essential, and thus if appropriate modifications in the economic system are made, individuals will no longer need to place the high value on hoarding that their elders still do. It should be possible, then, barring outright armed resistance by the vested interests, to meet the needs of the underprivileged primarily out of the expansion of the economy and of society rather than simply at the expense of those that already have. There is still among surprising numbers of the young a considerable compassion for the possessors of wealth, for they see the effects of enslavement to material conquest on the achievement of more fundamental human interests such as interpersonal affection and social harmony as well as individual autonomy. These young people wish to avoid this enslavement, but generally believe strongly enough in the principle of autonomy that they are inclined to allow the wealthy to continue so if they devoutly wish to and are willing to pay the human price.

The immediate objection to these remarks by those now in power will be that even if it applies to the critical sectors of American youth (which many of them will doubt, despite the likely evidence of it in their own privileged offspring), it cannot apply to the youth in the Soviet Union, who after all live in a society still largely backward economically in terms of consumer production and distribution. It is certainly true that the disparities between the two countries are drastic. But what matters more is the degree of internal change over time in economic production and distribution. The Soviet authorities are already protesting loudly that today's young people have lost the appreciation of the values of hard physical labor because they have had adequate material possessions handed to them by their elders and their system—precisely the charge made by many Americans to explain the discontent among American youth and offer a prescription for its removal by a return from affluence to labor. The point, therefore, is that the commonality between the youth in the two quite different countries is one of relative change rather than material, and that this relative-change-commonality should tend to create a similarity of attitudes and hence a bond between Soviet and American youth that spells trouble for maintenance of the now traditional hostility between the two countries.

But we must look still further to develop a satisfactory comprehensive understanding of what should prove a major determinant of significant change in international politics for the rest of the century. The impact of much greater knowledge of other people in other states coupled with the finding of remarkably parallel experiential situations of the young in different countries under different systems—a life under thermonuclear threat that shows no signs of abating, under systems characterized by industrialization and bureaucratization that exaggerate alienating work, depersonalization, and economic sufficiency—these conditions have offered the young not only an opportunity to conceive of better circumstances but also the incentive to seek changes that would offer greater opportunities for implementation of their own values of autonomy (especially where it does not preclude or curtail altruism) and increasing altruism (especially where it does not entail great self-sacrifice). But the most crucial impact of these changes—much exacerbated by the fact that they are common to the youth of both superpowers—is a weakening of strictly national boundaries. At the very time when the newer states are particularly concerned about developing nationalism and preserving boundaries in order to establish collective consciousness, and when the superpowers are finding themselves confronting major adversaries on borders that have come to mean much to them, the youth are looking for opportunities to relax the constraints to action and interaction that such boundaries have traditionally entailed. Thus we have a situation in which exhortation to heightened nationalistic consciousness is proving unable to overcome tendencies toward an emphasis on the importance of the inward life (through contemplation, drugs, and other approaches) and interpersonal sharing and harmony.

The concomitant emphasis is antimilitarist. The role of the military is viewed increasingly as retrograde, emphasizing and exacerbating differences with other states at the expense not only of world peace but also of the autonomous development of self-consciousness by youth so often asked to join the army and act against the drive for independence and autonomy manifest by other youths in foreign lands (or, in riot control, in their own land). The explanation for this antimilitarism is basically the combination of the decrease in nationalist consciousness and the fact that today's youth lacks the experience of a "good war" (as World War II seemed to most Americans) and lacks the cold war education in international relations of its elders. The combination of the heightened hostility that was the cold war with the recollections of a "good war" has led to the older generations to continue to embrace not merely the necessity of armed forces and their occasional employment, but further their therapeutic and beneficent effects on the social fabric. These arguments, whatever their validity in times past, are no longer convincing to most young people, who express and have often demonstrated their preference for doing their social service in the Peace Corps, VISTA, or socially relevant occupations such as teaching and community action.

Alert visitors to the Soviet Union have been impressed by the manifestations of these basic trends in youth attitudes and actions and by the ways in which the young are able to move underground in their expressions of them whenever the political climate proves repressive again. Thus the present observed trend backward toward something resembling "Stalinization" results in a voluntary curtailment or concealment of much of this ferment, just as the Soviet occupation has in Czechoslovakia. But the liberalizing developments are not ultimately reversible, except perhaps with the continuation and exacerbation of major external threat.

It is precisely because of this possibility that we must shift our attention to the People's Republic of China. American policy makers disquieted at the lack of public appreciation for the war in Vietnam when it was sold as a battle for the independence of South Vietnam attempted to shift the rationale to an effort to contain China, just as they sought to shift the rationale for the antiballistic missile (ABM) system from defense against the Soviet Union (which so many experts recognized as impossible, undesirable, or both) to defense against China. The reason for this is the still-primitive (in Western eyes) orientation and situation of the People's Republic of China, and the consequent possibility that deep-seated fears might be engendered or exploited by a return to the familiar "yellow-peril" arguments that so stirred the parents of today's rulers when they were in power. While this effort has not been notably successful in American youth, it may be more successful in the Soviet Union, which shares both a very long border and long-standing territorial and ideological disputes with China. Thus the possibility that China might serve, by its actions and the reactions of the superpowers, to obstruct if not undermine what otherwise seems to be a pronounced movement toward détente and perhaps even eventual cooperation is real and must be carefully considered and if possible averted.

The Chinese today constitute a nation still badly split on

virtually everything except appreciation of their heritage as the first civilized people. Part of the turmoil within China seems to be a manifestation of the inevitable political conflict of competing elites. A very important element of it, important to us as well as to the Chinese, concerns the challenge of developing and shaping a bureaucracy able to cope with and even encourage the drastic changes in society and government required by revolution. In addition, part of the turmoil seems closely tied to the debate over the attitudes and receptiveness of the external world—and especially the Soviet Union and the United States—to China's claim to preeminence in its geographical area. Although there is dispute on the point among Sinologists, most seem to believe that China's behavior is and always has been more Chinese than it is Communist. To the extent that this is true, it would seem likely to encourage the Soviet Union to make its peace with its older rivals in the West and thereby enable itself to devote greater attention and resources to its relations with the Chinese.

It is possible that, for geopolitical reasons and at the expense of once-alleged ideological commonality, the Chinese and the Russians will have to go through their own cold war before they are able to live with each other's commanding neighborly presence. Alternatively, the damping down of the American-Soviet cold war and the increasingly clear lessons of its cost in human suffering and social hypertrophy coupled with the increasingly positive and attractive example that these political giants can set in transcending these quarrels may offer an opportunity for greater efforts to incorporate the People's Republic into the international political community not as an outlaw but rather as a traditional state with much to offer in cultural wealth, political acumen, and lessons in dealing with the stubborn problems of bureaucracy and underdevelopedness politically and economically. This is an optimistic forecast, problematic at best. But the alternative of continuing confrontation and occasional explosion is pernicious enough to encourage both the United States and the Soviet Union to pursue such a possibility with attention and material resources.

Some very important questions remain following this examination of the changing attitudes of youths who are likely to be succeeding their elders in power, not only in middle-level bureaucratic positions, but ultimately in positions of major power—and who will, of course, increasingly comprise the major articulate constituency of those in positions of power in the interim. The first of these key questions is just how international, or perhaps more accurately multinational, this development is. There is good evidence of similarity in both attitude and relative position of youth not only in the superpowers, but also in all the significant industrialized nations of the West, including those in Eastern Europe. The fact that such attitudes can come to characterize youth in long-standing Communist states and especially the Soviet Union seems to suggest that its appearance should be expected in those Eastern European states still generally characterized as Stalinist.

The second key question is, of course, What will happen to these views and contacts as these youths age? Traditionally, youths have held youthful (primarily distinguishable from elderly) views only until they had the opportunity to enter the system as fledgling members, and then have turned into virtual replicas of their elders. Thus the question is generally put, What reason is there to believe that today's youths will retain some approximation of their youthful attitudes as they age and enter the system more fully? There are various indicators that this will be substantially true. First, many of the youths who have already entered the system, both in business and the professions such as law and teaching, remain significantly alienated and do not seem willing to wait their turn in receiving responsibility and power (a willingness that has always been the hallmark of those entering the system in the past). Furthermore, many of the youth of today are in significant ways stigmatized already by their youthful activities—some through arrest and jail records for civil rights, antiwar, antidraft, and drug "crimes," others with at least a shared sense of temporary community with others in these ventures—in ways that the system shows no signs of rewarding or even accepting. This common bond that distinguishes them from the others adds to a feeling of solidarity with those younger still and makes the youths more likely to continue to act in ways suggesting that they do not reject this past.

We may also expect continuation of such attitudes to be fostered by the continuation of the thermonuclear threat (something elders were not born with and hence may expect to disappear) and the surging of interest in and commitment to the urban and racial struggles, which is allowing youths to enter the establishment on the fringes and continue to pursue these interests. These are among the most salient of the major factors that suggest that these attitudes should well outlive the passage out of youth of most of those distinguished by them, and hence that their influence on the system will merit continuing attention.

The third question is not so easy to answer: How will the new youth—those succeeding the presently emergent youth—think and act? Should we expect more of the same, a new departure, or a return to the conventional evanescence? These youths seem even more sensate in their orientation (primarily because of the great emphasis on drugs, not just by youth but even more by the repressive society in which they find themselves) and hence inclined to greater privatization than their immediate predecessors. If their predecessors begin to achieve some decentralization of the authority structures in society, this should enable them to continue in this direction. The

most likely development, then, will be a growth of deference
in the new youth to the presently emerging youth who share
a concern with extending autonomy for the individual. Thus
today's emergent youth may well prove a key transitional
brief generation holding the proxy of its successors and hence
all the more powerful in its role in reshaping the political and
social world.

The Significance of These Tendencies

These possibilities could be greatly elaborated—
and perhaps should be in view of the prima facie impressive
case for their likelihood and the obviously great impact they
are likely to have on the political life not simply of the nation
but of the rest of the world. But two key considerations must
be emphasized. First, they are speculative, and should not be
accepted as highly likely without further examination, development, and testing over a brief future time. And second, the
analysis and proposition that precede and will follow them
here are almost entirely independent at this point in time of
the accuracy of this forecast. It is certainly true that, should
this forecast prove basically accurate, the recommendations
made above will be all the more important and at the same
time all the more inevitable (although their timing and their
exploitation will still be subject to alteration by far- or short-
sighted leadership). But should this forecast prove inaccurate,
there is still both opportunity and good reason for undertaking our program of reform of world politics. Indeed, should
the forecast prove inaccurate, the argument for the reform will
be all the stronger because of the increased threat to the survival of our present system posed by widespread discontent
and alienation confined within the existing political system.
The result of such inevitable conditions in the absence of an
evolution approximating that forecast in these pages could
only be catastrophic explosion. The survival of the system,

both nationally and internationally, in the face of this catastrophe laid onto the urban racial turmoil and the international thermonuclear peril could call survival into grave question. In the meantime, it is up to all of us. What can we do?

chapter eleven

The Conscious Construction of Our Future

Human action, we know, is based both upon one's perception of the conditions or circumstances in which one acts and upon one's understanding of (or, more accurately, beliefs about) effective action—beliefs that could be termed one's "theory of the world" or of the relevant chunk thereof. This theory functions as an assumption, although at least for some people it is an assumption open to revision when the failure of one's actions seems to indicate that the theory, rather than the perception of the situation in which it was applied, was in error. This distinction between perception of the situation and assumption about reality or about the limits and promising strategies of effective action is important—indeed crucial—for the study of behavior. And if it is clear and generally observed when we study individual behavior—especially that of children, whom we correctly assume to be engaged in the process of learning the nature of the world, of reality—it is not always clear when we study the conduct of collectivities —perhaps because so few decision makers articulate their assumptions about effective strategies, and because those who do so assume that their assumptions are correct.

Learning in Foreign Policy and International Politics

Even this notion of correctness of assumptions is often misleading. It is accurate in the case of the child attempting to discover how to walk, or how to read—activities that occur the same way, are achieved by the same general strategies today as long ago. But it is emphatically not true in the instance of the child learning to relate to, and hence to influence, his parents. Anyone observing a child (at least a child other than his own) coping with his parents can see the process by which the child learns not only the rules of conduct or the limits imposed by reality, but also how those limits get established, or how his relations with his parents are determined and hence altered, both by the other apparently irrelevant experiences of his parents (which create moods, susceptibilities, desires, expectations) and crucially by his own conduct and the expectations and confidences or fears it engenders.

Put another way, a child learns that the reality he confronts at any given time must be coped with, cannot be ignored, but can be altered over time by his behavior. In short, and in social scientific language, he learns *transformation principles*. The same phenomenon can be observed in the student learning to function in the school, although it is less obvious there because the environment is basically so repressive, and the hostility to change among teachers generally so great, that less of this learning and its implementation goes on. What does take place (usually in the form of ways of "beating the system") is carefully concealed by the students who know that to the extent that it is revealed, efforts will be made to quash it.

International relations are, not surprisingly, much more

like school than like the primary family. Consequently, the learning process is less obviously in operation, and indeed consists much more in the rote learning of the schoolroom than in the trial-and-error exploration and creation of early childhood.

The learning that we can see is still generally simple-minded, manifest in assertions about the "domino theory" or the "lessons of Munich" (probably better represented as the "Munich Psychosis"). This learning is undoubtedly limited by the fact that it is necessarily bureaucratic rather than individual. In addition, it is slower, and its improvement is constrained, perhaps because the major powers see themselves as existing in a world consisting entirely of "children," and the other states, if they see the big powers as adults, find a generation gap as glaring and upsetting as that presently afflicting the American population.

Thus, by itself this learning process would not seem to promise much in the way of opportunities for changing international reality. And indeed it does not. A nation cannot behave like a child and tentatively and experimentally alter drastically the nature and hence the constraints of reality. But that reality is subject to alteration by behavior of its component actors. If nations were like children and the world were like the family, we could simply begin experimenting in a purely trial-and-error way to find a type of international relations that offered greater promise than our present form and keep experimenting until we found it, simply discontinuing whatever behavior proved dysfunctional. Unfortunately, however, the stakes in international relations are simply too high. Remarkable as it seems when one takes a somewhat detached view of the horrors that so continually result from our extended playing of what could be termed "the old international politics," almost no experimentation will be countenanced, or no recommendation for experimental variation of

American (or any other major state's) foreign policy will be accepted by the policy makers, unless it offers overwhelming promise of success or at the very least threatens but little disruption of affairs should it fail.

This again, from another viewpoint, is the reason for the failure, or more accurately the irrelevance, of the traditional transformation recommendations such as world government, international law, and disarmament: they promise much but they threaten even more should resort to them fail, and they do not provide impressive accounts of the stages by which they could be implemented any more than they provide built-in hedges against failure. We are thus reminded of what we have all along known: any recommendation for significant change in American foreign policy must have several key features beyond its vision of a new world politics: it must carefully prescribe the various stages by which it is to be achieved; and it must include safeguards that will limit damage, should it fail, to acceptable levels—levels commensurate with the risk acceptable given the promise of the proposed new order.

Of course, we knew these essential features, even as we knew that behavior is significantly affected by, and reality potentially altered by, the assumptions one makes about the nature of reality within which one operates. But, unfortunately, most efforts to propose a new foreign policy for America fail to take explicit notice of these considerations, just as they fail to exploit the opportunities for changing constraining reality. The reason for this limitation seems as obvious as it is lamentable: it is hard enough to develop and pursue adoption of a new foreign policy without complexifying the task by delving into ways to alter the constraints of present reality incrementally and hence acceptably.

An important part of this complexity is the collective nature of most foreign policy making. Most analyses of international relations see the state as the actor and personify it, speaking as if the state itself acted. This is a convenient fiction, for it enables us to abstract from the bureaucratic politics that occur prior to a state's action, as well as from the idiosyncratic features of the individuals involved in the decision process. Obviously the abstraction enables us to analyze the interaction between states neatly. But this approach also has several grave drawbacks.

First, the personification of the state hardly facilitates relevant policy criticisms and suggestions. What recommendation state-as-actor analysis does allow must take the form of "the state should do X." Anyone with even remote acquaintance with governmental policy making knows how irrelevant such suggestion is. President Kennedy is widely reported to have told one adviser who made such a suggestion: "That's an excellent idea; now let's see if we can convince the government to do it." Governments and states do not do things, people do—people deeply enmeshed in institutions and surrounded by other people, each with some often rather unclear responsibilities and competences. And with the exception of a rare "idea whose time has come," a recommendation addressed simply to a government, that it do X, will rightly be seen as unhelpful and often irrelevant as well.

This does not mean that we cannot or should not make such general recommendations, but rather that we must be certain that they are based upon an understanding of the personal and interpersonal bases upon which individuals make policy and take action cooperatively (and conflictually) for the state. And this in turn requires that we delve into the world of the individuals involved, or at least into the mental structures of the decision process, before we recommend.

Only then can we avoid the difficulty of so many contemporary efforts of analysis and recommendation. Analyses based upon the study of the behavior rather than the experience of individuals—upon what someone does rather than upon the meaning of that action to the individual who takes it—do not enable us to understand the human basis of the action. Only if we base our analysis on the *experience* of the individual will we be able to speak to him (or to another individual in a similar situation) in terms meaningful to him about what he can and cannot do, as well as about how the way he conceives of or "images" a situation will affect what he believes the alternatives to be, and (taking the analysis the crucial step further) how the way he conceives or images the situation will affect the situation itself over time. How, in other words, he constructs reality in his mind, and how his mental constructions of reality will create reality in the world.

In fact, of course, these activities are subject to considerable influence by constructions of other persons and by processes of cumulation that constitute collective decision making. The conceptions and assumptions of others, if they are salient to the individual for some reason, may shape his own in the same way that any socially widely distributed knowledge affects one's way of thinking about some problem. This effect will be exacerbated when the decision in question is enmeshed in a policy hierarchy, as of course it will when the policy maker himself is enmeshed in a policy-making hierarchy. And of course, in addition, these images of others, these conceptions and assumptions held by others who are also involved in policy making, will be important because these others act in accordance with them, and hence generate or maintain their own segment of reality. And this complicates our analysis precisely because foreign policy decision making is in fact collegial. It is collective decision making.

Efforts to shape a recommendation that can be impressive or compelling to an individual participating in collective foreign policy decision making must be cast in terms of the position he should take. If he is urged to support a particular policy solely on its merits, the result may be surprising. For such decisions, because they are collective probably in small-group terms and certainly in hierarchical or serialized terms, are a fertile ground for *strategic thinking*. The outcome of the decision process will likely be some function not simply of the merits of proposed policies, but also of the bureaucratic and charismatic qualities of those involved and further perhaps of the decision process itself (in the way that the agenda and the rules of parliamentary procedure obtaining can so often crucially influence legislation, say, by the Congress).

These reminders of things most analysts know are important not simply because they may be of use to those "lobbying" on the making of foreign policy, but also because they suggest another way in which reality (in this case a policy) is created by men but can be more consciously created —its creation better controlled—if participants in the creative process are aware of this and can think strategically about it.

The personification of the state as actor in foreign affairs thus raises the danger that our understanding of the foreign policy process will be less likely to be accurate and will be much less amenable to influence by the most important inroad into change: the dispositions and reality image of the participating individual and his subsequent influence upon others involved. Thus, although for reasons of efficiency and clarity we will generally find it essential to speak in terms of states and their policies and actions, we must remember, when we reach the point of recommending new departures, that our states are composed of individuals whose reality images can vary just as their experiences and their responsibilities will. Nonetheless, we can find much consistency in reality images, and much that we regret about world affairs is heavily influenced by this consistency.

From Image to Policy

Conventional wisdom holds the resort to force to be not only an essential and even permanent feature of international politics, but a constructive feature as well, contributing to the stabilization of world affairs and the protection of freedom. Arguments over exactly why the resort to force is permanent and essential vary somewhat, but always incorporate the assertion that all or most states will continue to seek to have their own way in allocating resources (land, wealth, prestige, and whatever else they may desire) that are essentially scarce, and will view their own achievement of such scarce goods as important enough to justify not merely depriving others of these goods but also running considerable risks of major loss through organized violence when the others do not agree. Those conventionally wise therefore recommend that the United States, unless it wishes to lose what it has and all opportunity for further gain, reconcile itself not only to a world of gross disproportionality in welfare and freedom, but also to the occasional necessity to participate in violent quest of its objectives. Eternal vigilance and insightful advice should then make it possible for the country to pick and choose its violent encounters somewhat to its own advantage.

Faced with a choice between the incredible because highly optimistic and not very specific Idealist prescriptions and these somber but apparently well-reasoned analyses of the Realists, most Americans, and virtually all policy makers, have adopted one or another variant of the Realist analysis, and have recommended and acted accordingly.

One of the major intellectual folk-heroes of the conventionally wise, along with Machiavelli, is Thomas Hobbes, who discoursed at length in the seventeenth century on the ugliness of life in a "state of nature" in which there was no sovereign reigning over all, and nothing else served to constrain men in considerable privation and understandable fear from doing their worst to each other. It is certainly true that international relations—at least in the more virulent periods such as the world wars, the cold war, and probably the age of Vietnam and Czechoslovakia (which may just be the latest phase of the cold war)—has often appeared to resemble this dire account.

But we must not allow ourselves to be too impressed by this. What is striking is not that international relations are necessarily this way, but rather that they have remained this way despite a number of developments that might have been expected to alter them in our favor. Significant among these are: (1) the development of greater experience on which to learn how to avoid past errors and disasters; (2) the proliferation of scholars and advisers whose prime concern is international relations and who must be credited with hoping to help to avoid the worst and the horrible if they can; (3) the development of nuclear weapons and ICBMs and related advanced weapons systems that have made it quite clear that major war among major powers not only cannot be won impressively, but cannot even be survived impressively; and (4) the occurrence of Vietnam, which has finally led many to question the facile view that American military competence could prevail wherever we should choose to deploy it, at least if it were retooled for the area. For despite what the military would have us believe about its not having a fair chance in Vietnam because it was shackled (rather like Hitler's army claiming the same because it was not allowed to use chemical and bacteriological warfare), it has had a very fair test of its capabilities in the sorts of conflicts that are most likely in the Third World, and it has proved unable to master its tasks sufficiently even on the battlefield, let alone in strategic planning, given the constraints that seem likely to be imposed in and by any such conflict.

One would think, then, that these various developments —especially the greatly expanded reservoir of experience from which to learn and the striking facts of the worsening impacts of force and the decrease in effectiveness of force as used except for sheer destruction—would have led us to be highly skeptical of the entire worldview out of which the Realist analysis has developed. But instead, the sorts of revisionist thinking and prescribing we are now increasingly encountering begin by taking that Realist claim about the inescapability of force for granted, and then ask, in effect: Given the horrible quality of international relations and our effective impotence in gaining our ends by the use of force elsewhere around the globe, what can we do for a foreign policy? The answer, not surprisingly given the way the question is formulated, is: cut back on our involvements so that we are less often tested and hence can less often fail, and may even be able to succeed in some places through application of the principle of concentration of forces (so impressively demonstrated in the saturation bombing of many segments of North and South Vietnam, or in search and destroy missions in the South). There is no evidence to support that recommendation, and our past experience to confound it.

It could be, of course, that the world we live in does not allow for constructive international relations no matter how insightful our analysts, advisers, and policy makers are or may become. But, to look with even greater perspective, most of the previous massive challenges to the human race (except perhaps mortality itself, and we are still working on that) have proved to be surmountable, and that fact alone should encourage us to try harder than we have to uncover grounds for redirecting our efforts internationally.

The question then is, If we tentatively reject the Realist analysis in its many variants and the Neorealist prescription of simple withdrawal, is there or can we develop another approach to the understanding of the necessities and the possibilities of international political relations?

The Bases for an Approach to an Alternative

Realizing that we construct our own reality, although only in combination with other actors and in the context of the material realities that constrain all actors, when we notice that we are not succeeding as well as we might wish, or indeed as well as the theory on which we are operating suggests we should be, we appropriately ask the cause of our lack of success. Part of it might be the divergence of our conception of reality from those of others. But actually, both the United States and the Soviet Union seem to be acting on the same basic conception of reality. Indeed, we have suggested, this seems to be a significant part of the problem, in that the theory promises the education of the adversary but the operant principle produces his similar reaction leading to stagnation at best and drastic destruction rather frequently.

What then might we do to improve our lot? All we have to work with immediately is American foreign policy. Presumably we could change our own assumptions and hence our policies and actions. But we can and would do so only if we could find a viable and preferable alternative theory of foreign policy applicable to the problems of the United States today and tomorrow. We then ask, of course, whether our adversaries can be changed, since they today share our paradigm and our Realist conduct. Can the adversary be educated about the possibilities for change and then induced to cooperate?

In view of these considerations, an alternative to the

Realist view must (1) promise a significant improvement in international relations (the objective with which we assume we begin our quest) in terms of our values; (2) be able to entice adversarial cooperation increasingly; (3) recognize the "material" limitations and facilitating conditions set largely by technology and economy and important especially for their likely impact on the speed with which changes promised by some alternative that meets the two previous conditions might be expected and achieved.

Developing an alternative reality image that meets these criteria, of course, requires a very careful and extensive understanding of international politics. Among the key factors that must be realized and coped with are these. First, because at least two parties will be involved, there must be a recognition of the basic inviolable interests of these states. The key interests here should prove to be shared desires to avoid major war and stabilize dangerous threats that could promise only to draw the major powers into quarrels where there is little to gain even from success (and much to lose otherwise). Furthermore, it may be argued—in substantial part because of the importance of economic and social development to the attainment of such stability—that the parties share an interest in improving the lots of others when this is not too costly to them. The implication here might be crudely expressed as acceptance by the well-off of the normative implications of the principle of "Paretian optimality" according to which changes are acceptable and desirable if they improve one party's situation without diminishing that of any other (a principle to which we shall return shortly).

Furthermore, we must recognize those material conditions that are critical. The first is the impact and implications of technology, not only as it is devoted to war production where, barring unexpected progress in novel defensive systems, most innovation is destructive, but also as it serves to advance capacities for economic and other development. Such economic factors are the other major material factor requiring notice, and the significant fact here is the tremendous expansion that has occurred in the past to surpass our fondest expectations and may therefore be possible to engineer in the future to meet the needs of the less privileged in the world.

The second major factor of which we must be aware and about which we must be imaginative is the nature of interaction among states. We must bear in mind the above analysis of the types of interaction and remember which sorts of interaction require expansion if we are to improve the nature of international relations, as well as whatever we can learn about grounds for belief that such improvement is possible and about ways of engineering it.

Third, we must remain aware of the process of reality creation in international politics and attempt to structure our efforts to exploit its possibilities, rather than simply to attempt to innovate in a way doomed to failure because it does not delve deeply enough into these processes and the assumptions that often determine them.

And fourth, given the nature of international relations, our desires for change, and these three categories of relevant knowledge, we must be well aware of the requirements for constructive reciprocation-inducement in designing our innovations and of the importance of providing safeguards against the otherwise likely consequences of failure should the alternative approach prove unsuccessful.

The Basis in Reality

All analysts of international relations in the postwar years have recognized that deep-seated conflict between the superpowers forms the basis of relations, and most have understood the operation of the reaction process by which conflict is reciprocally escalated by the responsive competition or competitive action by each party. This phenomenon is most clearly manifest in the arms race, in which one side increases its arms not to a point to match development by the other, but either to achieve a momentary advantage or at least to attempt to cover or protect against an expected reaction by the other side; and then the other side indeed further increases its arms, again not just to equal the increase of the adversary, but to surpass it. This phenomenon continues in an upward spiral that knows no natural equilibrium and few occasional hesitations.

This process, and the underlying dynamic of it arising out of each side's defining the acceptable minimal strength not in terms of certain possessions but rather in terms of relative superiority—something that clearly cannot be possessed by both sides at once and is therefore rarely possessed by either for any length of time—this process is now well understood as it is manifest in arms policy, if even little is done to attempt to control the process and thereby limit the pronounced dangers to survival as well as to stability that develop from its maintenance.

Interestingly, research on the interaction of the superpowers in the years since the end of the Second World War has shown that the dynamic is also operative in the so-called nonsecurity areas such as education, foreign aid, economic development for internal consumption, space, etc. In other words, in these times each party to the international military struggle also acts similarly in response to, and anticipation of, the adversary's advances in areas not immediately related to military and political relations. The impact of this dynamic in the nonstrategic area has been mixed but pronounced. Thus, to take the most obvious instance, the Soviet successes with Sputnik led not only to drastic intensification of American space programs, but also to massive new emphasis on the teaching of science and math in the high schools—an impact that has extended not only to the lives of students forced to work harder but better trained for an increasingly technological and quantitative economic society, but also to the social sciences, where pressures toward quantification of approach and research have resulted as much from the increased competence and inquiries of young students as they have from the natural evolution of an infant science away from the intuitionistic and qualitative toward the quantitative.

The same effect can be seen in programs in other areas such as military alliances (in which the Warsaw Pact, virtually a carbon copy of NATO, was established when the United States and its allies decided to admit West Germany to NATO); multinational economic organizations (in which the Soviet-created Council for Mutual Economic Assistance or Comecon is the counterpart of the European Economic Community or Common Market), both of which are examples of response in kind.

The same effect can also be seen in the response in degree in education, scientific research, propaganda, and competition for allegiance and alliance of the nations of the Third World. Indeed, as pioneering research by Jan Triska and David Finley has demonstrated, there seems to be no area deemed of any significance by either superpower in which this phenomenon of "multiple symmetry-maintenance" is not clearly operative. Regardless of who takes the initiative, the other attempts to match it, and usually to match it in such a way that a dynamic of escalation occurs.

There are several explanations for the persistence and even strengthening and extending of this phenomenon of multiple symmetry-maintenance. First, each side seems to fear that any initiative by the adversary, while it appears to be in a nonsecurity area such as education, will ultimately turn out to have been crucial for security (as education is for advanced research and development capability). Second, each party by now has a learned habit of combativeness which encourages it to respond in such a mimicking way to any interesting adversary initiative, partly because relations have always (in the years since 1945) been conducted that way, and partly because each side has always in this period assumed the adversary to be malicious, so that any action it takes is aimed ultimately at undermining the other. But a third element in the explanation is probably equally important although perhaps less immediately impressive: the combination of an assumption that any action by an adversary requires a response, with a lack of imagination on the part of the major policy makers in each responding state, so that the most likely response is almost automatically aping the other. This has certainly been the case in much military development and in considerable parts of our foreign aid programs, even in cases where it has been rather obvious that the action of the initiator is not significantly promising.

For our purposes the important point in this brief examination of both security and nonsecurity policies and behaviors of the major adversaries is that there continues to exist a pattern of symmetrical response with frequent escalation of intensification, and that this dynamic which has been found here may exist in more pronouncedly political international relations and may therefore be exploitable there as well as in military and nonsecurity competition.

The evidence for its existence in political interaction— beyond the rather obvious instances of foreign aid and propagandizing—is not so easily found. But there are two ways in which it can be discerned. One is to examine relations between the United States and the Soviet Union in the summer and fall of 1963, during the time from President John F. Kennedy's " Strategy for Peace" speech at the American University commencement in June 1963, his assassination that November, and the period of transition following it. One scholar, sociologist Amitai Etzioni, has termed this period "The Kennedy Experiment" because it was one in which a distinct effort was made to relax relations, establish and maintain (at least briefly and perhaps shallowly) a détente, and do so through the taking of small but carefully designed initiatives.

The other way to approach evidence for the existence of symmetry-maintenance in political relations is to examine not an instance of constructive peace-oriented innovation, but rather instances of the converse: actions by one party that worsen not only relations between the superpowers but also the whole international climate, and that are then in perceptibly similar ways replicated by the adversary. The most fruitful period for examination here is probably that opened after the collapse of the Kennedy-Khrushchev détente by the drastic expansion of American involvement in Vietnam, beginning with Johnson's decisions to commit American troops to ground combat and American air power to the bombing of North Vietnam (the latter undertaken the very day that Soviet Premier Kosygin was in Hanoi). This American action, which caused considerable problems for the Soviets in their relations with their "fraternal Socialist allies" in North Vietnam and with Communist states around the world because of the running contest for international Communist leadership with the Chinese, was followed in the spring of 1967 by much increased Soviet meddling and encouragement of disorder in the Middle East culminating in war, and then the following year by the Soviet invasion of Czechoslovakia. Both of these major departures in Soviet policy, each contributing significantly to the pollution of the international climate, were facilitated by the impact of the American involvement in Vietnam, not only because that involvement made the positions of Soviet progressives more difficult and strengthened the hand of the militarists in the Kremlin, but also because the American actions made it easier for the Soviets to conduct and succeed at actions otherwise increasingly difficult in the present years, just as the British-French-Israeli actions over Suez had so facilitated the crushing of the Hungarian revolt in 1956.

The Nature of an Alternative Reality Image

In view of these features of contemporary patterns of international relations, what will be the necessary and promising nature of an alternative reality image for foreign policy making? The theoretical assumption to be made as a substitute for the Realist assumption of an adversary single-mindedly and all-resourcefully hostile to us and our system will have to be a belief that each party is aware that neither party is happy with the threatening state of international relations, that each realizes that it is in the situation together and inextricably with the other, and that each has alternative demands on itself domestically that it would prefer to be able to cope with without the continuing massive diversion of both attention and resources to largely self-defeating ventures in military buildup and conflict.

Furthermore, the assumption will include, as another part of its "factual" assertion, recognition that material scarcity and especially that of an economic (production and distribution) sort is actually declining in the international economy. This is a complicated assertion and one that is not at all obvious. It is quite clear that demand for these resources expands continually, but much of that demand is of two sorts: military and Third Worldly. Were there not the same hypertrophic military demand, each major power could meet its own needs largely out of its own resources and have surplus resources that could be directed to the needs of other elements in the world economy. And thus, in this sense, the traditional concept of scarcity is relevant not in consumption goods but only in land itself—something of which there is actually plenty until states find themselves in competition for political and military preeminence around the world. The importance of this analysis of international economic scarcity is, of course, that the postulation of such scarcity has long been a crucial part of the Realist analysis (as the motive for, or at least the impelling material constraint that drives states to major conflict) and a part that has been self-fulfilled because it is accurate in a world of hypertrophic military consumption. But if the world were otherwise, scarcity would rapidly turn into plenitude for the major industrialized states and a tremendous opportunity for economic development in other areas that would redound to the increased benefit of all. This point must not be lost sight of despite its utopian air.

The alternative "theoretical" assumption (the assumption about effective action opportunities) that couples with these assertions about basic material and political reality is the contention that the way to improve the nature of international relations is to recognize these material facts, adopt the ethical argument underlying the principle of Paretian optimality (that a change that does not harm anyone but helps someone is desirable) as a criterion limiting the immediate aggrandizement of the rich and allowing employment of surplus in the poor areas, and then design and undertake policy initiatives which will (if the analysis is correct, the time propitious, and the policy well-executed) overcome the resistance of the adversary and induce reciprocation and contribute to the gradual creation of a new international political reality—the world transformation capitalizing on the operating principle of multiple symmetry-maintenance where this is required, and on the residual good will and eternal hope of most of mankind wherever it is available.

What then might be done to alter American foreign policy so that relations with the Soviet Union could be improved in the ways we have contended are desirable? Most contemporary and historic criticisms and recommendations have suffered from either too little or too much recognition and acceptance of the existence of conflict between major powers. The nature of this conflict has, over the years and with the drastic changes in technology and economy, shifted considerably from the material to the ideational. The conflict is now much more an attitude than a substantive material dispute, and it resides much more in a basic assumption of malevolence by each party than it does in flagrant geopolitical confrontations, even though there remain exceptions to this generalization, most clearly those in Vietnam and in Central Europe.

As we recognize the existence—and the likely continuance—of this basic conflict and attempt to understand its nature and its malleability, we should find it desirable to continue to exploit the existing tendency toward multiple symmetry-maintenance as it is manifest in nonsecurity competition. This will have the advantage of allowing venting of the competitive tendencies that are so prevalent in man while having beneficial effects internationally (through foreign aid, competitive trading, exploration and development in the seas and outer space, etc.) and domestically (through education, economic development, and other programs) if the programs are designed carefully and imaginatively.

The success or failure of the program and the policy based upon it will be determined primarily by actions taken on security matters, both military and political. Responsive relations in these areas have generally been counterproductive of desired improvement in international relations. This will not be true of measures taken to create and strengthen détente by defusing tension areas and improving communications and personal interaction among the major powers. But in those areas in which there remain political disputes with territorial bases and in those aspects of relations heavily dependent upon military procurement and deployment (in the arms race and its constituent policies)—in other words, where there are material bases to disputes and hence overlapping interests and conflicts—there should be opportunities for bargaining interaction, in which each side gives something and gets something. Precisely what is given and gotten will be much less important if the political climate is improving, for most of the significance of disputes over territory (such as Berlin) and over weaponry (such as ABM or size of strategic missile forces or warhead size and quantity) arises from the underlying assumption of unending pervasive conflict rather than the values of the possessions at issue. In other words, square mileage in Central Europe or overkill capability assumes overwhelming importance only when what is most important is having more than an adversary and flaunting it to justify the costs of getting or holding it and to convince the adversary that he is indeed worse off for your possession.

There will also be opportunities for responsive interaction in the military and political sphere. These will arise in instances of competition in the Third World—where those nonwhite states continue to allow intervention, meddling, or constructive actions by the primarily Caucasian superpowers —and relaxations in superpower restrictions on personal interactions of their populace and foreigners, as well as in matters of arms control and international trade in strategic materials. Such competitive and responsive interaction will be more likely than explicit, organized bargaining, especially in areas involving lower-level elements of the countries (such as trade among firms and industrial combines), as well as areas in which exact correspondences are difficult to work out and hence less formalized and less measured equivalences can be engineered by responsive relaxation of restraints, reductions of weapons procurement rates, development programs, or deployment. The chief problem in such nonbargained responsive relaxation and reduction will be the credibility of the good-faith proclamations or postures of the states involved in the face of, or with the background of, the long-standing assumption of malevolence on each side. Another term for this problem, somewhat less accurate but more understandable, is *trust*—the difficulty any state will find in trusting the deeds and their significance even given surveillance or other reconnaissance information confirming the actual steps taken. Thus the early stages of creation and implementation of such a program of improvement will be particularly difficult and require perseverance.

However, we already know much about how to design the measures and present them to adversary and domestic populations so that they will be impressive and offer good grounds for trial given anything but the most ferocious and festering fear and aggressive assumptions. Furthermore, there is good reason to expect great progress in the design of measures once we begin devoting more attention and imagination to such programs as we have so long done for strictly military measures. Of course, the design of the technical features of a given measure of arms control or foreign aid will be heavily dependent upon the substance of the material and behavior to be controlled, purveyed, or otherwise involved. We cannot say much about such measures without being highly specific, and such specificity must be tailored not only to the state of hardware and behavior at the time the measure is proposed but also to the stage in the process of deescalation or devolution at which it is to be introduced.

Nonetheless, we can say several important things about the features of the program, within which these measures will reside and find significance, to be emphasized in presenting it. In this country at this time, the greatest favorable impact is likely to be achieved by noting and emphasizing the potential domestic impact of reallocated resources freed by the novel policy. These resources do, of course, include money. But at least as important they include as well attention and imagination on the part of policy makers presently devoting themselves primarily to a contest with an adversary rather than directly confronting the ultimately transcendent problems of world economic development, population control, and the design of authority structures able to achieve the control required for progress without at the same time losing contact with locally felt needs and also curtailing individual autonomy.

In addition, these resources include the participation and enthusiasm of young people. Ultimately, whether for good or for ill, the greatest impact of the Vietnam imbroglio seems likely to prove to be on the young people, who have been in large measure alienated from the political system that has produced such a policy, proved unable to reverse it when all good sense to them and many others seemed to urge that, and asked that they do the sacrificing in attempting to salvage something out of the situation. There were long times when young people willingly accepted such decisions and compulsions, perhaps because they anticipated with equanimity eventually succeeding to power (where today many seem to doubt whether the elders will preserve the world long enough to allow them to succeed, or at least whether there will be anything worth preserving once those now young do get power), or perhaps because they had been impressed with the legitimacy of political authority (where today the young and others know too much about the failings of authorities to have much unquestioning confidence in their legitimacy). But if there were times when the young could be coopted without a struggle or at least without considerable reservation, those times are now all but gone. The world will probably be the better for this new development ultimately. But whether or not that is true is almost irrelevant, for what is presently required is ways to regain the confidence and employ the developing expertise of the young in the service of improving international relations. And a program of the sort outlined here holds the most promise of that.

One way of increasing its appeal to the young as well as to others is to emphasize the domestic impact of reallocated resources. We are all well aware now of the great pressures on national resources that are limited in scale because of the tax policies of the federal and other governments. If resources, both money and attention, are increasingly freed for domestic employment, considerable improvement of the lot of minorities and the poor generally could be engineered, at least if imagination as well as material resources were shifted to such problems from national defense. Similarly, it should become possible for us to confront, as a society, the emerging problems of highly industrialized or (as many are now terming it) "postindustrial" society—especially those of opportunities for significant political participation and meaningful work, which are problems that we do not yet see the solutions to, but that we are increasingly realizing must be solved if we are to be able to preserve our system that is supposedly both "capitalist" and "democratic." Furthermore, we should be able significantly to improve the economic development of the country, both by coping with long unmet regional needs and by finally gaining some significant control over the inflation that is so intensely stimulated by the production of those consumption goods par excellence, war materiel, rather than appropriate capital goods.

This is not the place for a comprehensive account of either the benefits to be expected from a drastic transition from a warfare state to a postindustrial civilian state, or the ways in which such benefits could be engineered through the design of decreasingly military programs and consumption. Only those blinded by their own vested military interests could question the proposition that the country and the world would be much better off were we able to shift from such a warfare posture to a peace posture without substantially increasing risk of serious war threatening to our vital interests at home and abroad.

But this is, of course, the rub and the reservation. For those actively interested in the survival of the warfare state, as well as a great many who are not, have not yet been convinced that there is any promising alternative to our present militaristic approach to international relations and national security—beyond perhaps a Fortress America policy of virtual isolation that would not really promise either security at home or pleasure about the eventual fate of the rest of the world. We and the militarists both recognize and agree that isolationism is not the answer. This is a world of heavy interdependence extending far beyond military "security" arrangements to economic ties and ideological wishes for the fortune of other peoples. And this nonmilitary interdependence is not only very difficult to escape but commendable for its impact in expanding our horizons concerning alternative designs of social organizations and political relations.

Where the resistance comes, both from the vested-interest militarists and from those of us who have become their ideological adherents, is on the question of military-political security. If we could become convinced that an alternate plan promised greater or even equal security, we could convert. Part of this problem has long resided in our semiconscious requirement that an alternative not only offer greater benefits but also offer greater certainty of attainment of those benefits. In other words, we have not been willing to take an equal or greater expected risk for greater benefits rather than our present high risk for lesser benefits. This arises partly out of the human proclivity for any sort of present certainty (even a certainty of misfortune) over uncertainty, and partly out of the institutional bias for system maintenance regardless of its effects and promise. Thus we must overcome both institutional inertia and the social tendency to insure rather than gamble, if we are to be able to engineer a significant transformation in American foreign policy.

But in a sense this emphasis on uncertainty and risk overstates the problem. For there are some good and impressive reasons for believing that the program proposed here does offer great promise. The design of the program and its rationale to emphasize the impact of reallocated resources domestically should itself have appeal to (and hence encourage envy in if not immediate replication by) the Soviet Union. For as we well know, the Soviets have all the economic problems we have and then some, and further they have increasing problems with their geographically concentrated and hence more dangerous national minorities than we, as well as the same increasing ferment among their youth. Thus a significant part of the program required should consist in efforts to educate the adversary—the Soviet Union, both leadership and citizenry—about the opportunities they would be foregoing should they attempt to capitalize on the first significant initiatives we might take to break the vicious militaristic circle.

Such educational efforts must be coupled with an increase in our perseverance, so that our initiating measures might have time to improve the climate for reciprocation or replication by the adversary by overcoming the expectable skepticism about our credibility as well as the benefits of whatever acts we have demonstrably undertaken. But we must at the same time see that we avoid taking action to increase or intensify involvements that are retrograde. The chief difficulty here will be temptations to continue our military definition of the status quo and defense of the status quo ante in areas of the world where popular resistance to tyranny is emergent —as we have in Vietnam and the Soviet Union has in Czechoslovakia. Each of us has opportunities for continuing such action that are virtually boundless as newer states become increasingly turbulent and rambunctious. But we must convince ourselves of what Vietnam has taught us about the undesirability of such involvement in fundamentally intractable situations.

One fortunate thing about such learning is that it afflicts not only the United States, as a result of its involvement in Korea, Laos, the Congo, and Vietnam, but also increasingly the Soviet Union as a result of its involvement in the Congo, Cuba, the Middle East, and almost certainly Czechoslovakia.

But we are well aware, especially as a much-involved superpower, that a policy of disengagement and demilitarization of relations with the Soviet Union and refusal to become militarily involved with tumultuous troublespots in the Third World will not suffice as a new foreign policy for the United States. Our continuing relations with that Third World, and especially the Middle East which will offer increasing temptation, a failure to come to terms with the People's Republic of China (especially given her intensified quarrel with the Soviet Union and her opportunities for mischief with her other neighbors), and persistence in our efforts to keep Western Europe well aware of the proximity of the cold war—these other crucial aspects of our present international posture and relations could of themselves easily defeat and destroy efforts to improve relations with the Soviet Union in the way outlined above, and probably would do so very quickly were we not to have developed as well significant new approaches to these countries, areas, and their manifest challenges. Thus we must also develop policy guidelines for our relations with the rest of the world as we attempt to exploit the tendency toward multiple symmetry-maintenance in creating a new international reality in which to relate to the Soviet Union. But fundamental change in Soviet-American relations is and will remain the keystone in the reconstruction of international relations, for the superpowers set the example and often as well the language and the terms of trade out of which international relations in our era are collectively constructed.

Testing the Alternative

We found in our examination of the operational testing of the Realist theory that it was subject to massive failure because of the excesses to which reaction processes pushed confrontation of a military and hostile political sort, and that the best that could be hoped from it, if all went well, was stagnation and deterioration.

Our alternative has not yet been tried in any *comprehensive* way. We do have, as has been indicated, bits and pieces here and there to suggest reasons for some optimism about its success (especially findings of the extensiveness of the operation of the principle of multiple symmetry-maintenance in nonsecurity matters and the experience of the "Kennedy Experiment"). And we know well that if the prospects for the world and its people under the continued dominance of the Realist theory are as bleak as they seem today and the promises of the alternative theory are as great as they seem today, such a new departure should be well worth a try. The losses from a failure of carefully designed innovation would probably be minimal. The gains from successes in re-creating international reality would be almost incalculably great.

This alternative shares with the Realist theory two very American and traditional features: an optimism about the prospects for the human race, emphasizing the hope that man can learn and profit from his experience; and a claim that the United States, foresighted and enlightened, could lead the way. But it has several features that distinguish it as an intellectual product from the Realist view. First, a much greater consciousness of the way in which cognition affects reality—

the way in which we create reality by our theoretical assumptions as well as by our actions. And second, a better understanding of the nature of interaction processes and the ways in which they in their turn constitute international reality and provide the raw material out of which that reality may be restructured.

It is by the unification of the original pragmatism of the Realist and this developing sense of the role of cognition in reality creation coupled with understanding of the place that interaction patterns play in constituting reality that this alternative offers some hope of significant improvement in international relations in accordance with the overwhelming changes in both material conditions and ideological predispositions that are now emerging in the advance guards of so many states. What is now required is emergence of greater perceptive and imaginative analysis by scholars unashamedly committed to the improvement of the nature and substance of international relations for others as well as for Americans and willing to do the extensive work that must underlie and inform the development and design of this or some other alternative to the dominant reality image. Reality itself, of course, might ultimately deny success to such an alternative image. The tragedy at present is that general acceptance of our conventional conception of reality seems to preclude its development, and the reality that this conventional conception tends to generate will not allow its testing.

chapter twelve
Some Conclusions About the Challenge

The proposals that eventuate from this analysis are not revolutionary in the sense that they have never been made before. Various scholars and occasional statesmen have proposed one or another or even some combination of the policies and attitudes suggested here, and various scholars have engaged in careful study of multinational interaction designed to increase our understanding of patterns of interaction and their dynamics. But comprehensive effort to unite scholarly analysis and policy proposition into a coherent and defensible theory of national policy opportunities has unfortunately not yet been made.

This study offers, in a sense, a design for a composite and developed version of such an unusual if not new theory of international interaction—or perhaps more specifically, a novel hypothesis about international interaction and a comprehensive worldview or reality image in terms of which to apply that hypothesis to test its validity. Such a reality image is a way of viewing the world and understanding the past as well as coping with future situations of practical decision problems. Any individual always has such a worldview when he makes or recommends policy, but the worldview is usually tacit rather than explicit, often self-contradictory when examined explicitly, and rarely well tested when it is applied.

Our image of national interaction suggests and tends to substantiate, by its comprehensiveness and consistency as well as the applications we have made to past and present international political situations, a drastically altered United States foreign policy designed to improve significantly the longer-run achievement of interests of the United States and the rest of the world.

The view or reality image presented here has not, of course, been tested adequately. The study of American-Soviet interaction which finds multiple symmetry-maintenance characteristic of those relations since 1945 is of great significance, as is the application of the model to the study of the so-called Kennedy Experiment of 1963 which seems to confirm the promise of the venturesome approach to shifting toward détente from aggressive confrontation that is proposed here. And the explanation in terms of the principles of interaction of the series of misfortunes and disasters which international politics have incorporated from 1945 to the present, culminating most recently in the Vietnam imbroglio, the Middle Eastern war and continuing crisis, and the Czechoslovakia invasion, merits careful thought and further application.

But more, we require mapping of past interaction to show the high degree of responsiveness not only to military action and to nonsecurity matters, but also to political competition in crisis after crisis, and, perhaps ultimately more significant for the future of the explanation offered here, of political cooperation where it has come to exist despite the generally unfavorable political context within which such small gains toward stability and détente have had to be brought about.

Furthermore, and of greatest importance, we need venturesome and carefully planned testing of the hypothesis that such new departures as are recommended here will be reciprocated—if the initiatives are carefully designed to meet the exigencies of each geographical area and political problem with a sensitive understanding of the overarching complex international system and especially its structure of relations which are to be affected (turned toward peace) by the initiative in combination with other similar initiatives and with protective measures maintained and taken as required but as remotely as possible from the major ventures so as not to outweigh or discredit them.

It is not really a question of whether or not we will discover and understand adequately the basic mechanisms of interaction among states and how to deal with them in the service of improvement of international relations. For surely, barring a cataclysmic and universally undesired major nuclear war, we shall eventually. Their nature becomes increasingly clear from crisis to crisis, as the opportunities for improvement promised by their understanding also do. The real question is *when* we will learn of these factors—who will make and recognize the discovery and who will apply the greatest imagination in understanding and then employing that understanding to initiate the major "peace race" that men have long dreamed of. But several other questions of considerable import too remain.

The first is whether we shall learn these facts soon, or whether their learning will require further great pain such as that inflicted by the Vietnam situation and promised for the asking in the rest of Southeast Asia, Latin America, Africa, the Middle East, and perhaps even Europe as well.

And the second is whether we shall learn these things efficiently. Many of those now learning from the drastic misfortune of our present policies are learning the lesson of withdrawal and isolation. Some will eventually come to see that isolation, far from sufficing, will probably prove very dangerous, and will then come to embrace the theory of constructive responsive interaction offered here and endorse policies based on it. But this learning of isolation is a learning out of desperation, and the subsequent learning of these views will also be out of desperation. Few things are done well in sheer desperation, and learning about international relations is surely no exception. So the question is whether we shall come to examine, test, and if it works adopt, a view such as this with urgency but not with desperation, or whether we shall ignore it until desperation makes us learn it expensively and bitterly.

For if we do not learn it soon enough, the effects as well as the causes of the major transformations in individual, national, and international affairs that are already emerging will be well upon us. And if that is the case, the problems will be greater and the necessary change even more drastic than would be the case today. Such massive changes and greatly increased threats are always difficult to conceive, and always difficult to implement and cope with.

The difficult challenges of such conception and coping can be best understood as the creation of insight and policy guidelines, the innovation of policy programs, and the education of the public at large.

Policy Creation

The creators or developers of policy must first free themselves of preconceptions arising out of the education we have all received at the hands of the cold war and its apologists and out of the belief that continued total confrontation of adversaries is always essential, even in this radically new technological age. They must then become more willing to consider undergoing *different* risks in new departures. Such risks may be of a magnitude similar to those we now endure, but they might well appear to be greater because they will be less familiar. They must be risks that offer greater promise of reconstruction that will result in a new and better world politics.

These creators and developers of policy must also come to view international relations as a complex whole, as a system, and must therefore continually seek ways to understand its complex interactions and exploit opportunities this interrelation provides for synergistic improvement.

Policy Innovation

The case of the policy innovators—those in government service and on its advisory fringes—is somewhat different. Unfortunately, in the uncertain world of compound risks in which we live, those in authority tend almost without exception to overestimate the difficulties of change and to be pessimistic about the possibilities for success of any new departure. Thus, they are least likely to welcome proposals for change if they are well informed about just what obstacles can be foreseen to its achievement. The requirements of change seem to be, first, knowledge of some obstacles and ways around them, and second, ignorance of some obstacles so that the entrepreneurs may act as if those obstacles are not there and thereby overcome them despite what would be, if known, grounds for pessimism. The innovators must not become depressed and rendered immobile by recognition and contemplation of the great galaxy of possible obstacles that seems at the time to exist. Their image of the obstacles must be such that, while acting to implement change and cope with the obstacles to it that they do realize, they will construct a new reality in which some of the unrecognized obstacles can disappear so that the system is transformed in ways unanticipated as well. The implications of this generalization about the attitudes and susceptibilities of the entrepreneurs of ideas in government (or, for that matter, in business) might appear to be that all-knowing analysts and creators deceive or at least conceal from their innovators. And perhaps that might prove a wise policy were it to prove possible—which seems quite

unlikely. Rather, the implication of import is that we as analysts and recommenders should spend less of our attention
on possible obstacles and more on program development and
the devising of strategies for implementation. In that way, we
may all be a bit less aware of all the possible obstacles, but
we may also be less immobilized and more inclined to venture
change, and hence almost certainly more successful.

Public Education

The case of the public at large, or at least the
politically relevant because mobilizable public, is still more
difficult. There can be no question of informing it, for the
public would spot change in any event were the change significant, especially in a country with the widespread and relatively free if not always imaginative press that the United
States has. And the public will be especially important in a
country featuring frequent elections because great fear could
emasculate the policy innovations by threatening electoral
castration of venturesome politicians and their diplomats and
constrained soldiers.

The question is, really, one of information strategy. The
public must be informed, but that information should be in
terms of progress achieved rather than debate over program.
The significant lesson of the Kennedy Experiment in 1963—a
lesson learned almost immediately by a rather timid executive
branch and a fearful military—was that the American people
have a strong capability to be led to fear of change, but they
also, especially in times of prolonged crisis and discomfort
such as these, have a remarkable capacity to do an about-face
and endorse any significant measures that seem to promise a
start toward relaxation of tensions and return of attention to
more geographically contiguous problems. Thus the public
shifted, according to polls at the times, from opposing a
nuclear test ban to supporting it because they saw signs of

progress in diplomacy and heard expressions of hope from their leaders, and were themselves watchfully waiting for an opportunity to endorse progress. This phenomenon can also be seen in recent changes in public attitudes toward an opening toward China, and in general would almost certainly be even stronger today, with the increasing attention being paid to our long-range domestic difficulties and their frequent critical uprisings. Thus careful emphasis upon domestic benefits promised by international transformation coupled with statements of progress rather than simple invitations to the debate over program de novo or from conventional presuppositions should make such ventures acceptable and even highly desirable to most of the American people.

The Prospects and the Promise

But what if these optimistic instructions for a strategy of innovation are not followed, or worse, what if the situation in which they would become relevant does not arise because the leadership is not receptive to proposals for significant change in the assumptions we make about the nature of international reality and the intransigence of our adversaries, and hence in our policies for international improvement?

The sorts of policies designed and proposed in this essay are largely volitional. They offer opportunities for anticipating major new developments in the international system and exploiting and guiding them in directions favorable not only to international relations in general, but also to America's constructive role. In ways that will make these new approaches more promising of effectiveness, those underlying changes cannot be reversed by American and Soviet recalcitrance. Many of the factors cited throughout this study are factors that will be strengthened as inevitable trends in states and their relations develop further. We have found that it is much easier to uncover the existence and immediate movement of such trends than it is to forecast their most likely development in the coming decade or more of international relations and come up with a comprehensive vision of the nature of the international system and its operation in, say, 1980. Nonetheless, there are, as we have seen, important things to be said about those significant major developments, and while their magnitude is not always clear, their nature and direction usually are. Major new developments in the international system will have drastic and ominous implications for "world politics as usual."

The widening unhappiness with most of what presently constitutes international relations is already sufficient to lead large numbers of Americans to advocate the remarkably desperate "solution" of curtailing our presence and action in vast sections of the world that contain most of the world's people, most of the entangling problems, many of the major challenges to the continuation and extension of human life on earth—and, we should also recognize, much of the potential insight into the enrichment of the quality of our lives and society that our domestic turmoil and fear suggest that we need.

Are we then, at this most critical of times, to leave the rest of the world just as we reach the moon, and to run the grave risk that life on earth abroad and at home will come more and more to resemble what we have found in our heavens? Our imaginations can do better. And in the last resort, it is our imaginations that create our social world. It is time for us to devote our resources of attention and imagination and energy to the task of developing a new American foreign policy that will enable us to move from the politics of the cold war and Vietnam toward a New World Politics.

A Note on Sources,
Influences, and
Further Pursuits

One of the major pleasures of having written a book—beyond that of having at last finished it—is reflecting upon its relations to the efforts of others and seeing its ineluctable dependence upon the work of so many others (and the strength it derives from this) as well as its significant departures from what has come to characterize the field.

Newton was widely believed to have originated the remark, "If I have seen farther, it is by standing on the shoulders of giants"—at least until Robert Merton revealed the plenitude of shoulders upon which Newton's remark rested (see Merton's splendid book, *On the Shoulders of Giants: A Shandean Postscript* [New York: Free Press, 1965]). An author is rarely conscious of the height, and is often only aware of the knobbiness, of his terrain while he is at work, for he constantly finds instances in which no one seems even to have understood the problem, let alone solved it helpfully, and from his perspective those others he sees seem often to be pygmies whose shoulders, when they are visible, appear to be slippery slopes to the Bog of Conventional Wisdom.

Of course, much of this *is* appearance rather than reality, and it is a pleasure, at the conclusion of what long seemed like a Sisyphean effort, to acknowledge one's major debts—particularly as they may entice those who have borne with the author this far to move on to exploit further the helpful work of others, hopefully in the same constructive quest.

The essential elements of arms control I have examined comprehensively in *Arms Control in International Politics* (New York: Holt, Rinehart & Winston, 1969).

By now, the matters of diplomatic history that occupy much of chapter 2 should be relatively common knowledge and require neither scholarly substantiation nor further reference. Still I want to mention, as particularly helpful to me, Selig Adler's *The Isolationist Impulse* (New York: Abelard, Schuman, 1957) and Norman Levin's *Woodrow Wilson and World Politics* (New York: Oxford University Press, 1968).

I have not relied here on the fascinating and important work of contemporary revisionist historians because I have not been concerned with the ascription of blame for the cold war, but rather impressed by the commonality of view—particularly on the efficacy and essentiality of the resort to force and its threat—of both parties, and the way in which this commonality has constructed and maintained as the dominant social reality the cold war we know so well and lament so much.

Close cousins, perhaps, of the revisionists are those I have termed "Neorealists," who argue for commitment cutting. They have played an important historical role in calling into question the disposition of our forces, and although I believe they have not yet delved deeply enough into the causal processes of international politics, I by no means denigrate the importance of such reconsiderations as Senator J. W. Fulbright's *The Arrogance of Power* (New York: Vintage, 1966), Ronald Steel's *Pax Americana* (New York: Viking, 1967), and Theodore Draper's *The Abuse of Power* (New York: Viking, 1968), as well as Hans Morgenthau's various recent reconsiderations.

The problem of explaining international political developments and the foreign policies that constitute them will doubtless continue to plague us. I have quite extensively discussed this matter, and cited various candidate approaches and some of their authors, in a previous book, *International Political Analysis* (New York: Holt, Rinehart & Winston, 1969). Among the more recent additions to this literature are Graham Allison's *The Essence of Decision* (Boston: Little, Brown, 1971) and Richard Barnet's *The Roots of War* (New York: Atheneum, 1972). There will certainly be others, and they will often be welcome.

The general theoretical approach I increasingly find particularly helpful, that version of the sociology of knowledge often termed "reality construction," has an important ancestry in the works of Alfred Schutz—the most important of whose writings are now available in Helmut Wagner's edited collection, *Alfred Schutz on Phenomenology and Social Relations* (Chicago: University of Chicago Press, 1970). For my purposes, the two most important general developments upon this work are Peter Berger and Thomas Luckmann, *The Social Construction of Reality* (Garden City, N.Y.: Doubleday Anchor, 1966); and Burkhart Holzner, *Reality Construction in Society* (rev. ed.; Cambridge, Mass.: Schenkman, 1972). Also helpful are various of the permutations on "ethnomethodology" that can be found represented in H. P. Dreitzel, ed., *Recent Sociology #2* (New York: Macmillan, 1970) and certain of the collected essays of anthropologist Gregory Bateson entitled *Steps to an Ecology of Mind* (New York: Ballantine, 1972). But this field is only beginning to burgeon.

The analysis of social processes remains remarkably underdeveloped, largely because categorization and analysis must depend upon one's original objective. The definition of "process" from the *Oxford English Dictionary* (Oxford: Oxford University Press, 1933) can be found in volume 8, page 1403. Particularly helpful in various respects is Kenneth Boulding's seminal study, *Conflict and Defense* (New York: Harper & Row, 1957). Boulding's influence on this study has been considerable.

Reality images have also been grossly neglected. Remarkably, when Kenneth Boulding argued in 1956 in *The Image* (Ann Arbor: University of Michigan Press, 1956) that images mattered, it was a pioneering insight! There are by now some helpful studies, especially Dean G. Pruitt's article, "Definition of the Situation as a Determinant of International Action," which appears in Herbert C. Kelman's edited collection, *International Behavior: A Social-Psychological Analysis* (New York: Holt, Rinehart & Winston, 1965) along with some other interesting and relevant studies, and which is reprinted in David V. Edwards, *International Political Analysis: Readings* (New York: Holt, Rinehart & Winston, 1970). Also relevant is Thomas Halper, *Foreign Policy Crises: Appearance and Reality in Decision Making* (Columbus, Ohio: Merrill, 1971).

Among important studies relating to questions concerning perception besides Pruitt's are Joseph De Rivera, *The Psychological Dimension of Foreign Policy* (Columbus, Ohio: Merrill, 1968); Robert Jervis, "Hypotheses on Misperception," in *World Politics* 20 (1968): 454–79; and a great many psychological studies, many of which are cited in these works.

The classic work on the self-fulfilling prophecy is Robert Merton's, to be found in his collected essays entitled *Social Theory and Social Structure* (rev. ed.; New York: Free Press, 1957). An interesting application to education is Robert Rosenthal and Lenore Jacobson, *Pygmalion in the Classroom*

(New York: Holt, Rinehart & Winston, 1968). Important general works on the image of the future include F. L. Polak, *The Image of the Future* (2 vols.; Dobbs Ferry, N.Y.: Oceana, 1961), and Wendell Bell and James Mau, eds., *The Sociology of the Future* (New York: Russell Sage, 1971). An interesting application of some of this work on reality images and consciousness is Paulo Freire, *The Pedagogy of the Oppressed* (English trans.; New York: Herder & Herder, 1971).

Influencing others' images in interpersonal relations is the subject of much of the fascinating work of Erving Goffman, especially his first study, *The Presentation of Self in Everyday Life* (Garden City, N.Y.: Doubleday Anchor, 1959), *Strategic Interaction* (Garden City, N.Y.: Doubleday Anchor, 1971), and *Relations in Public* (New York: Basic Books, 1971). Also relevant here, although very limited in scope, is Robert Jervis, *The Logic of Images in International Relations* (Princeton, N. J.: Princeton University Press, 1970).

While the linkage between images and processes, and hence the question of how to exploit processes, has not yet received the attention it must have, some extremely stimulating preliminary work has been done by Kenneth Boulding— especially in his study, "Towards a Pure Theory of Threat Systems," in *American Economic Review* 53 (Papers & Proceedings, May 1963): 424–34. This and other relevant pieces are reprinted in David V. Edwards, ed., *International Political Analysis: Readings* (New York: Holt, Rinehart & Winston, 1970).

Among the more interesting and comprehensive programmatic efforts to design ways to such progress are C. Wright Mills, *The Causes of World War III* (New York: Simon & Schuster, 1958); Charles Osgood, *An Alternative to War or Surrender* (Urbana: University of Illinois Press, 1962); Amitai Etzioni, *The Hard Way to Peace: A New Strategy* (New York: Collier, 1962); Vincent P. Rock, *A Strategy of*

Interdependence (New York: Scribner's, 1964); and W. Warren Wagar, *Building the City of Man* (New York: Grossman, 1971). In bits and pieces, each of these works has a significant contribution to make to the program recommended here. And the theory underlying the work of Osgood and his program (called GRIT) is closely related to a major part of the theory developed here.

Speculation on the future is endemic these days, and there seems little reason to catalogue other such efforts. More interesting is what little methodological work exists. The greater part of this deals with technological forecasting, and most of this is summarized in Erich Jantsch, *Technological Forecasting in Perspective* (Paris: OECD, 1967). Other contemporary literature on forecasting can be found in the issues of two periodicals, *The Futurist* and *Futures*. And I have discussed problems, methods, and relevant literature in a chapter of my book *International Political Analysis* (New York: Holt, Rinehart & Winston, 1969).

The final chapters of the present book build not only upon what precedes them here but also upon aspects of what has preceded them in the social sciences. As I mention in the text, two studies by others are of special relevance and significance. They are Amitai Etzioni's study of "The Kennedy Experiment" which is chapter 4 of his book *Studies in Social Change* (New York: Holt, Rinehart & Winston, 1966); and Jan F. Triska and David Finley's "Soviet-American Relations: A Multiple Symmetry Model," in *Journal of Conflict Resolution* 9 (1965): 37–53, also reprinted in David V. Edwards, ed., *International Political Analysis: Readings* (New York: Holt, Rinehart & Winston, 1970). Anyone interested by the argument in the present study—and especially those skeptical about its potentiality—should profit from these two studies.

There are of course almost limitless works of relevance to one or another element of so broadly ranging a study as this. I have tried here to cite those either most influential on my work or most likely to help others pursue the questions of greatest centrality to this study whether or not I used or even had encountered them while at work on this book. No doubt others have influenced my work but escaped my mind; to their authors I apologize. There are certainly other individuals who have influenced my work more generally over the years. I have acknowledged this specifically in previous books and here shall only thank them once more without specific mention—which they well may find considerate, since my thoughts have by now diverged from, or even sometimes turned upon, many of theirs—I hope constructively. In this phenomenon lies some of whatever progress a developing field of study makes. And so I would expect and even hope that such will also eventually be the fate of this work.

> *I must Create a System*
> *or be enslav'd by another Man's.*
> *I will not Reason or Compare:*
> *My business is to Create.*

> —William Blake, "Jerusalem"

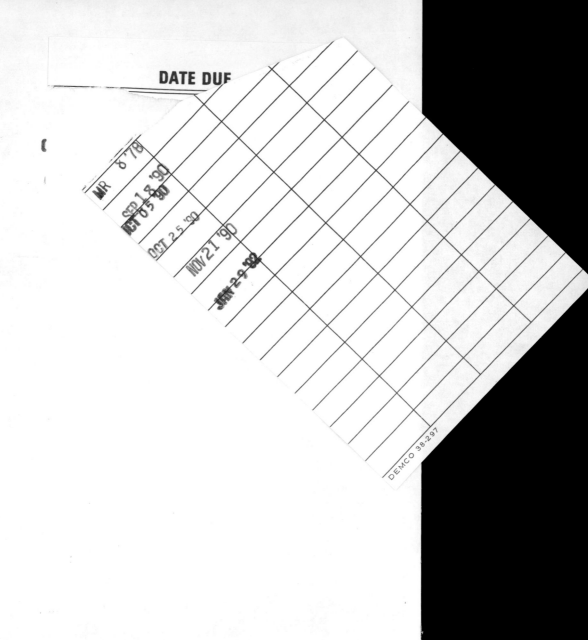